Lindsay Clandfield

Straightforward

Beginner Student's Book

MACMILLAN

Pronunciation	Reading	Listening	Speaking
Contractions (1)	Conversations: four greetings		Meet other students
		Introductions	Dialogue: introductions
Intonation (1) (wh-questions)		Four phone conversations	Roleplay: phone numbers
The alphabet		At the hotel	At the hotel
	Conversation: in a hotel room		Game: What's this in English?
/iː/		In a café	Roleplay: in a café
Consonants: /dʒ/, /d/, /r/ & /tʃ/	Emergency workers		Communication: Jobs
Contractions (2)			Game: Correct or incorrect?
	United Nations International School		
Word stress (1)		Conversations about age	Talking about how old things are
Schwa /ə/	Family album website		Talking about your family
		In a flat	Communication: Describe and draw
	World of work		Talk about where you live, work
Consonants: /s/ & /z/		Conversations about technology	Technology and you survey
Intonation (2): (yes/no questions)	Conversation with a man about his new job		Game: My new job
/e/, /ʌ/, /uː/ & /ɪ/	Morning people and night people		Talking about your daily routine
Connected speech (1)	Community Centre noticeboard	Phone call to community centre	Roleplay: a famous person's free time
	Eating habits survey		Make a healthy living survey

Pronunciation	Reading	Listening	Speaking
Word stress (2)	Weekend break		Presentation: a city you know
	Conversation about a neighbourhood		Communication: Two places
Consonants: /m/, /f/, /v/ & /p/		In a city	Roleplay: tourists in New York
Years	Remakes of television shows and films		Talking about films and TV Presentation about you in the past
	Story from a detective show		Find someone who ...
Intonation (3)		Conversations about opinions	Game: That's my opinion
	Email about a holiday		Talk about a place you went on holiday
Past tense regular verbs	Last concert of the Beatles		Retell the story of the Beatles
/θ/ & /ð/		National holidays	Interview about a national holiday
Diphthongs: /aɪ/, /eɪ/, /aʊ/ & /əʊ/		Conversation about the weekend	Guided conversation about the weekend
Connected speech (2)	Pub quizzes in Britain	A pub quiz	Make a quiz
	Shopping in London	In a shop	Shopping questionnaire Roleplay: in a shop
can/can't	What we can't do, what we can do		Game: The English Challenge
Consonants: /ŋ/		At a concert	Dialogues on the phone
	Britain's favourite paintings	Conversations about paintings	Describe a picture
Intonation (4)	Me and my mobile	Three phone calls	Guided phone call
		At the airport	Describe a picture Roleplay: at the airport
going to	Blog about the end of a course		Guided conversation – end of course

1A | Hello. Goodbye.

FUNCTIONAL LANGUAGE: greetings (1)

1 🔘 1.1 Read and listen.

Hello.
Hi. Goodbye.
Bye.

2 🔘 1.1 Listen again and repeat.

3 Say hello to other people in the class.

LISTENING

1 🔘 1.2 Listen to the conversations and point to the correct photo.

2 🔘 1.2 Listen again and read the conversations.

1
A: Hello.
B: Hi.
A: What's your name?
B: My name's Jack.

2
A: Goodbye.
B: Goodbye.

3
A: Hi.
B: Hello.
A: I'm … Orion. What's your name?
B: My name's Emily.

4
A: What's your name?
B: Willy
A: Goodbye, Willy.

FUNCTIONAL LANGUAGE: asking and saying names

1 🔘 1.3 Listen and repeat.

A: What's your name?
B: My name's Ben. What's your name?
A: I'm Emma.

2 Work in pairs. Ask and say your name.

GRAMMAR: *to be* (1)

Full form		Contraction
I am	=	*I'm*
What is	=	*What's*
My name is	=	*My name's*

> SEE LANGUAGE REFERENCE PAGE 22

1 Complete the conversations with *'m* or *'s*.

1
A: Hello. What (1) ____ your name?
B: I (2) ____ Thomas.
A: Hello, Thomas.

A: I (3) ____ Mr Smith. What (4) ____ your name?
B: My name (5) ____ Jessica.
A: Goodbye, Jessica.
B: Bye.

2 🔘 1.4 Listen to the recording to check your answers.

PRONUNCIATION: contractions (1)

1 🔘 1.5 Listen and repeat.

I am   I'm
My name is   My name's
What is   What's

2 Practise the dialogues in Grammar exercise 1. Use contractions.

SPEAKING

1 Walk around the class and meet other students.

A	B
Hello.	Hi.
What's your name?	I'm ... . What's ... ?
My name's ...	Goodbye.
Bye.	

ENGLISH AROUND YOU: names

1 🔘 1.6 Listen to some popular names in Britain.

2 Do you know people with English names? Which English names are popular in your country?

1B | Where are you from?

FUNCTIONAL LANGUAGE: greetings (2)

1 🔵 1.7 Read and listen.

A: Hello, Lucy.
B: Hi, Dan. This is Philip.
A: Nice to meet you, Philip.
C: Nice to meet you, too.

2 Work in groups of three. Practise the dialogue.

VOCABULARY: cities and countries

1 Match the words to the pictures.

1 Brazil
2 Italy
3 England
4 Russia
5 France
6 the USA
7 China
8 Germany

2 🔵 1.8 Listen to the recording to check your answers. Repeat the words.

LISTENING

1 🔵 1.9 Listen and write the names of the countries or cities you hear.

1 My name is Polly. I'm from _____.
2 This is Pierre. He's from _____ , _____.
3 Her name's Sofia. She's from _____.
4 His name's Michael. He's from _____.
5 Where are you from?
   We're from _____.
6 This is Nikita and Igor. They're from _____.

2 🔵 1.9 Listen again and repeat.

A Bejing

B Frankfurt

C Rio de Janeiro

D New York

E Rome

G Moscow

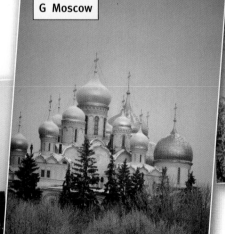

F London

H Paris

GRAMMAR: *to be* (2) (*my, his, her*)

Full form		Contraction
He *is*	=	He's
She *is*	=	She's
We *are*	=	We're
They *are*	=	They're
My name is …		
His name is …		
Her name is …		

> SEE LANGUAGE REFERENCE PAGE 22

1 Underline the correct form of the verb to complete the sentences.

1 I *am / are* Jennifer.
2 His name *is / are* George.
3 They *are / am* from England.
4 He *is / am* from London.
5 She *is / are* from Manchester.
6 We *are / is* from Russia.

2 Make sentences about the pictures.

Her name is Audrey Tautou.
She's from France.

Audrey Tautou, France

Valentino Rossi, Italy

Maria Sharapova, Russia

Ronaldinho, Brazil

FUNCTIONAL LANGUAGE: asking and saying where you're from

1 🔊 1.10 Read and listen.

A: Where are you from?
B: I'm from Milan.

2 Work in groups. Ask other students, *Where are you from?*

SPEAKING

1 Work in groups of three: A, B, and C. Complete the conversation with information about you.

A: Hi. I'm ____. What's your name?
B: Hello. My name's ____. I'm from ____. Where are you from?
A: I'm from ____.

A: Hello, ____.
C: Hi, ____.
A: This is ____. He/She's from ____.
C: Nice to meet you.
B: Nice to meet you, too.

2 Practise the conversation.

3 Close your books and practise the conversation again.

1c | What's your number?

FUNCTIONAL LANGUAGE: greetings (3)

1 🔘 **1.11** Read and listen.

A: Hello. How are you?
B: I'm fine, thanks. And you?
A: Fine, thanks.

2 🔘 **1.11** Listen again and repeat.

3 Work in groups. Say hello to the other people. Ask *How are you?* and answer.

VOCABULARY: numbers 1 to 10

1 🔘 **1.12** Read and listen to the numbers.

1 one **2** *two* **3** three **4** four **5** five **6** six **7** seven **8** eight **9** nine **10** ten

2 🔘 **1.13** Listen and say the correct number.

LISTENING

1 🔘 **1.14** Listen and match the conversations to the pictures.

A
Last call
623 485 531

B
English class 7pm

321 4510 –
Mrs Kirsch

C
James
945 0782

D
CALL NOW
1 888 962 962

2 🔘 **1.14** Listen again and say the numbers in the pictures.

FUNCTIONAL LANGUAGE: asking for and saying phone numbers

1 🔘 1.15 Read and listen.

A: What's your phone number?
B: It's 928 2914.
A: My phone number is 926 0438.

Language note

Say *oh* for *0* in phone numbers.

2 🔘 1.16 Listen and repeat the phone numbers.

1 687 054 265
2 44 0378 543 0157
3 350 2871

3 What's your phone number? Tell a partner.

GRAMMAR: *it*

My phone number is 966 0438. **It's** *966 0438.*
It's = *It is*
Use *it* for things.

> SEE LANGUAGE REFERENCE PAGE 22

1 Replace the words in *italics* with *he*, *she* or *it*.

1 Where is Mark from?
  Mark is from England.
2 *Mary* is from Glasgow.
  Glasgow is in Scotland.
3 What's her phone number?
  Her phone number is 753 891.

2 🔘 1.17 Listen to the recording to check your answers.

PRONUNCIATION: intonation (1)

1 🔘 1.18 Listen to the intonation in these questions.

How are you?
What's your name?
Where are you from?
What's your phone number?

2 🔘 1.18 Listen again and repeat the questions. Copy the intonation.

SPEAKING

1 🔘 1.19 Read and listen to the conversation.

Woman: What's your work number?
Michael: It's 350 2851.
Woman: OK. What's your home number?
Michael: It's 928 2914.
Woman: What's your mobile number?
Michael: Sorry, I don't have one.

Roleplay

2 Complete the chart with your phone numbers.

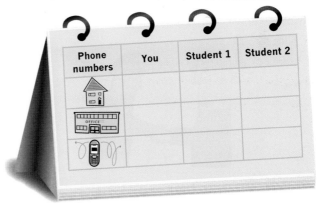

Phone numbers	You	Student 1	Student 2
🏠			
🏢 OFFICE			
📱			

3 Talk to two other students. Complete the chart with their phone numbers.

Useful language

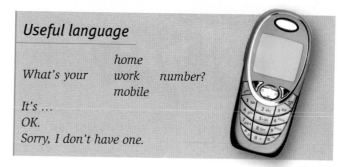

What's your ... home / work / mobile ... *number?*
It's ...
OK.
Sorry, I don't have one.

11

1D Review

FUNCTIONAL LANGUAGE

1 Complete the words to make phrases.

1

H___!

2

G___!

3

Nice to m___ you.

Nice to m ___ you, t___.

4

Hi! How a___ y ___?

I'm f___. And you?

F___, thanks.

2 🔘 **1.20** Listen to check your answers. Repeat the phrases.

12 |

READING & VOCABULARY

1 Read the text about three teachers and complete the chart.

Meet your teachers!

This is Will Goodfellow. He's from Sydney, Australia. His work phone number is 0465.

This is Sofia Galia. She's from Palermo, Italy. Her work phone number is 0468.

This is Olga Grau. She's from Germany. Her work phone number is 0470.

Name:			
From:			
Work number:			

2 Complete the chart with information about your teacher. Ask questions.

What's your name?
Where are you from?

3 Make a similar text about your teacher.

This is …

GRAMMAR

1 Complete the sentences with the correct form of the verb *to be*.

1 My name _____ James Bond.
2 I _____ from England.
3 They _____ Andre Agassi and Stefi Graf.
4 He _____ from Las Vegas, America.
5 She _____ from Mannheim, Germany.
6 We _____ the group, U2.
7 We _____ from Ireland.

2 Complete the sentences so they are true for you.

My name ....
I ... from ...
My phone number ...

3 Work in pairs. Read the sentences from exercise 2 to your partner.

SPEAKING

1 Work in pairs. Choose one of the pictures. Prepare a dialogue. Use the useful language to help you.

2 Practise your dialogue. Then present your dialogue to another pair in the class.

Useful language

Hello. / Hi. / Goodbye. / Bye.	
How are you?	*Fine, thanks.*
What's your name?	*My name is … /I'm …*
This is …	
Nice to meet you.	*Nice to meet you, too.*
Where are you from?	*I'm from…*

Self assessment (tick ✓)
In English …
☐ I can greet other people.
☐ I can introduce myself and other people.
☐ I can count to ten.
☐ I can say my phone number.
☐ I can say where I am from.

2A | The hotel

LISTENING

1 Look at the pictures. Where is it? What city is it? What country is it?

2 🔵 **1.21** Listen and check.

3 Who is at the hotel?

a) Tom and Emily   b) Tom and Katy   c) John and Katy

VOCABULARY & PRONUNCIATION: the alphabet

1 🔵 **1.22** Listen and repeat the alphabet.

ABCD EFG
HIJK
LMNOP QRS
TUV WXYZ

2 🔵 **1.23** Listen again and say the letters in groups.

/eɪ/	A H J K
/iː/	B C D E G P T V
/e/	F L M N S X Z
/aɪ/	I Y
/əʊ/	O
/uː/	Q U W
/ɑː/	R

3 🔵 **1.24** Listen and tick (✓).

1	Tom	Tim
2	Jen	Jim
3	Mike	Mack
4	Mary	Marie
5	Stephen	Steven

4 Work in pairs, A and B.

A: Spell names from exercise 3.
B: Point at the correct name.

5 🔵 **1.25** Look at the forms. There is a mistake in each name. Listen and correct the mistake.

1

Registration Form

First name: Tom

Last name: Cruise

Country: USA

2

Registration Form

First name: Victoria

Last name: Beckham

Country: England

FUNCTIONAL LANGUAGE: spelling names

1 🔘 **1.26** Listen and repeat.

A: How do you spell your *last name*?
B: C-R-E-W-E-S

2 Spell your first name and last name.

Roleplay

3 Work in pairs, A and B.

A: Choose one of the English (first) names from *English around you* on page 7.
B: Ask A how to spell the name.
Swap roles and continue.

VOCABULARY & LISTENING: numbers 11–20

1 🔘 **1.27** Listen and repeat the numbers.

eleven 11
twelve 12
thirteen 13
fourteen 14
fifteen 15
sixteen 16
seventeen 17
eighteen 18
nineteen 19
twenty 20

2 🔘 **1.28** Listen and complete with numbers.

	1	2	3	4
1				
2		Name	Room number	
3		Tom Crewes		
4		Mrs Bickham		
5		Mr and Mrs Woods		
6		Camilla Parker		
7				

Hotel Reservations — File Edit View Insert Format Help

SPEAKING

1 🔘 **1.29** Read and listen to the conversation.

Tony: Excuse me. I have a reservation.
Receptionist: Yes, what's your name please?
Tony: Tony Blare.
Receptionist: How do you spell your last name?
Tony: B-L-A-R-E.
Receptionist: Thank you, Mr Blare. You're in room 15B.
Tony: Thank you.

2 Work in pairs. Prepare a similar conversation.

Useful language

Excuse me.
Please.
Thank you.

ENGLISH AROUND YOU: acronyms

1 Read the acronyms. How do you say them in English? What do they mean?

2 🔘 **1.30** Listen and check. Read the tapescript on page 120.

3 Do you know any other English acronyms?

2B | Hotel room

VOCABULARY: common objects

1 🔘 **1.31** Look at the picture and listen to the words.

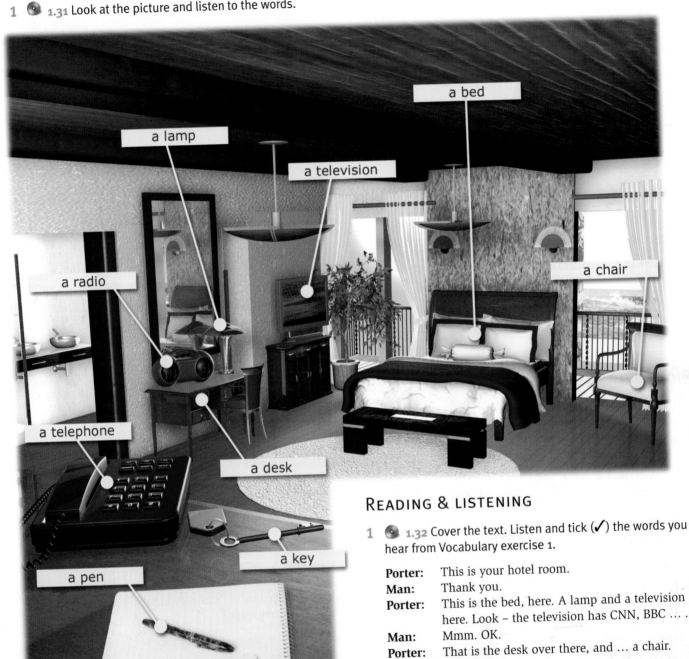

a bed

a lamp

a television

a chair

a radio

a telephone

a desk

a key

a pen

a notebook

2 🔘 **1.31** Listen again and repeat.

READING & LISTENING

1 🔘 **1.32** Cover the text. Listen and tick (✔) the words you hear from Vocabulary exercise 1.

Porter:	This is your hotel room.
Man:	Thank you.
Porter:	This is the bed, here. A lamp and a television here. Look – the television has CNN, BBC … .
Man:	Mmm. OK.
Porter:	That is the desk over there, and … a chair.
Man:	Thank you.
Woman:	Excuse me, what's that?
Porter:	That's … the radio.
Woman:	Oh. Thank you.
Porter:	This is your key.
Man:	Thank you. Here you are.
Porter:	Thank you!

2 🔘 **1.32** Listen again. Read the text and check your answers.

GRAMMAR: *this/that/here/there*

Here
> What's **this**?
> **This** is a + noun

There
> What's **that**?
> **That** is a + noun

The plural of *this* is *these*. The plural of *that* is *those*.
Use *these* and *those* with plural nouns.

> SEE LANGUAGE REFERENCE PAGE 22

1 Underline the correct word.

1

What's *this / that* in English?
It's a CD player.

2

What's *that / this*?
It's my phone.

3

Where is he?
He's *here / there*. In the hotel!

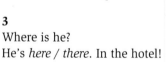

4

Is *this / that* your pen?
Yes, it is. Thank you.

5

Look over *there / here*!
Where?
It's Superman!

2 🔊 **1.33** Listen and check your answers. Say the sentences with a partner.

SPEAKING

1 Work in small groups. One student points to an object on the page or in the class. Ask *What's this/that in English?*. Another student answers.

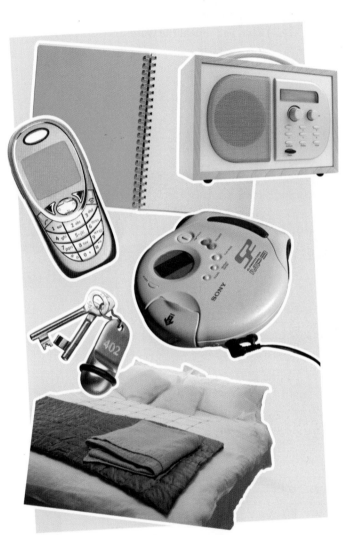

2 Take turns. Continue.

Useful language

What's this/that in English?
It's a …
I don't know.

2c | The café

VOCABULARY: food and drink

1 Match the words to the pictures.

> a coffee   a tea   a cheese/ham sandwich
> a croissant   an orange juice   an omelette
> an apple juice   a mineral water

2 🔘 1.34 Listen and check.

3 🔘 1.34 Listen and repeat the words.

A

B

C

D

E

F

G

H

LISTENING

1 🔘 **1.35** Listen to some people at a café. Tick (✓) the food on the menu you hear.

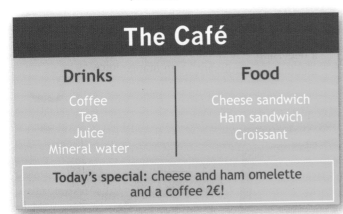

The Café

Drinks	Food
Coffee	Cheese sandwich
Tea	Ham sandwich
Juice	Croissant
Mineral water	

Today's special: cheese and ham omelette and a coffee 2€!

GRAMMAR: plurals, *a, an*

Use *a, an* with singular nouns.
a + consonant
  a sandwich
an + vowel
  an omelette
To make nouns plural, add *-s* or *-es*.
  two coffees
  two sandwiches

> SEE LANGUAGE REFERENCE PAGE 22

1 Add *a* or *an* to the words.

1 ___ orange juice   5 ___ croissant
2 ___ sandwich   6 ___ apple juice
3 ___ key   7 ___ bed
4 ___ chair   8 ___ desk

2 Choose the correct phrase or sentence.

1
a) Three coffee.
b) Three coffees.

2
a) A ham sandwich, please.
b) An ham sandwich, please.

3
a) I have two notebooks.
b) I have two notebook.

4
a) The omelette is two euro.
b) The omelette is two euros.

PRONUNCIATION: /iː/

1 🔘 **1.36** Listen to the underlined sound in these words.

ch<u>ee</u>se   th<u>ree</u>   pl<u>ea</u>se   coff<u>ee</u>   sp<u>ea</u>k

2 🔘 **1.37** Listen and repeat the sentences.

1 Three teas and three coffees.
2 These are your keys.
3 Excuse me, please.

FUNCTIONAL LANGUAGE: in a café

1 🔘 **1.38** Listen and repeat the dialogue.

A: I'd like a sandwich, please.
B: Would you like cheese or ham?
A: Cheese, please.
B: Here you are.

2 Work in pairs. Turn to page 119.

Roleplay

3 Work in pairs, A and B.

A: You work in the café.
B: You are the customer.

Prepare a conversation.
Use the functional language
and the menu to help you.

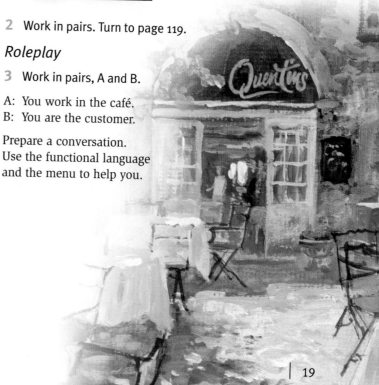

2D Review

FUNCTIONAL LANGUAGE

1 Put the conversation in order.

	Clunie.
1	Hello.
	Thank you.
	Hello. What's your last name?
	C-L-U-N-I-E.
	How do you spell your name?

2 🔘 1.39 Listen and check your answer.

3 Work in pairs. Make a similar conversation.

LISTENING

1 🔘 1.40 Listen to four conversations. <u>Underline</u> the correct spelling of English place names.

1 Canbridge / Cambridge
2 Torquay / Torquee
3 Cheshere / Cheshire
4 Greenwich / Grennich

2 Do you know any strange place names? How do you spell them? Tell a partner.

VOCABULARY

1 Match the words in the box to the objects in the picture. There are three extra words you don't need.

a key   a bed   a chair   a desk   a pen
a television   a notebook   a phone   a lamp
a coffee   a croissant   an orange juice

2 Work in pairs. Cover the words. Test each other.

What's this in English?
It's a phone.

3 Complete the Bingo cards.

Bingo card A: write six numbers between 1 and 20.
Bingo card B: write six letters between A and Z.

A

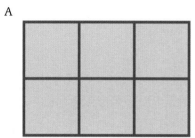

B

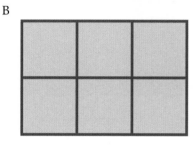

4 Play *Bingo*. Your teacher will explain the rules.

GRAMMAR

1 <u>Underline</u> the correct word to complete the dialogues.

1
A: Hello.
B: Hello, I'd like two ham *sandwiches / sandwich,* please.
A: Two *sandwiches / sandwich.*
B: Yes, and *an / a* orange juice too, please.
A: Here you are. *One / Three* pounds, please.
B: Thank you.

2
A: Hi, I'm Martin.
B: Hello Martin. This is your *desk / desks*.
A: Good.
B: This is your chair. Your phone is here, and *a / an* lamp
  … here.
A: Thank you. My key?
B: Oh, yes. Here you are. Two *keys / keyes* for you.
A: Thank you.

> **Self assessment** (tick ✓)
> In English …
> ☐ I can spell words.
> ☐ I can count to twenty.
> ☐ I can ask what words are in English.
> ☐ I can ask for a drink or food in a café.

GRAMMAR

Verb *to be*: present simple

Full form		Contraction	
I am		I'm	
You are		You're	
He is	from the United States.	He's	from the United States.
She is		She's	
It is		It's	
We are		We're	
They are		They're	

It

Use *it* for things.

What's your phone number?
It's 9328 2289.

Other contractions

What is your name? → *What's your name?*
That is the hotel. → *That's the hotel.*

My, his, her

My name is Adrian.

His name is Jack.

Her name is Paula.

Here, there, this, that

Here

What's this?
This is a table.

There

What's that?
That is a chair.

A, an, plurals

Use *a*, *an* with singular nouns.

a + consonant

a sandwich, a table, a chair, a country

an + vowel

an omelette, an apple juice

To make nouns plural, add *-s* or *-es*.

Two coffees, three sandwiches, phones, keys

These, those

The plural of *this* is *these*.

This pen. These pens.

The plural of *that* is *those*.

That key. Those keys.

FUNCTIONAL LANGUAGE

Greetings
Hello./Hi.
Goodbye./Bye.
How are you?
I'm fine, thanks. And you?

Asking names
What's your name?
My name's … (Jack). What's your name?
I'm … (Tania).

Meeting people
This is … (Philip).
Nice to meet you.
Nice to meet you, too.

Asking where you are from
Where are you from?
I'm from … (Germany).

Asking phone numbers
What's your phone number?
It's … (928 2914).

In a café
I'd like a sandwich, please.
Would you like cheese or ham?
Cheese, please.
Here you are.

WORD LIST

Countries
Brazil *n*	/bra'zɪl/
China *n*	/'tʃaɪnə/
England *n*	/'ɪŋglənd/
France *n*	/fraːns/
Germany *n*	/'dʒɜːmənɪ/
Italy *n*	/'ɪtəlɪ/
Russia *n*	/'rʌʃə/
the USA *n*	/ðə juːes'eɪ/

Numbers
one ***	/wʌn/
two ***	/tuː/
three	/θriː/
four	/fɔː/
five	/faɪv/
six	/sɪks/
seven	/'sevən/
eight	/eɪt/
nine	/naɪn/
ten	/ten/
eleven	/ɪ'levən/
twelve	/twelv/
thirteen	/θɜː'tiːn/
fourteen	/fɔː'tiːn/
fifteen	/fɪf'tiːn/
sixteen	/sɪk'stiːn/
seventeen	/ˌsevən'tiːn/
eighteen	/eɪ'tiːn/
nineteen	/naɪn'tiːn/
twenty	/'twentɪ/

Objects
bed *n****	/bed/
chair *n****	/tʃeə/
desk *n****	/desk/
key *n****	/kiː/
lamp *n***	/læmp/
notebook *n*	/'nəʊtbʊk/
pen *n***	/pen/
phone *n****	/fəʊn/
radio *n****	/'reɪdɪəʊ/
television *n****	/ˌtelə'vɪʒən/

Food & drink
apple juice *n***	/'æpl ˌdʒuːs/
cheese **	/tʃiːz/
ham *n*	/hæm/
sandwich *n**	/'sænwɪtʃ/
coffee *n****	/'kɒfɪ/
croissant *n*	/'krwæsɒŋ/
mineral water *n****	/'mɪnrəl ˌwɔːtə/
omelette *n*	/'ɒmlət/
orange juice *n***	/'ɒrəndʒ ˌdʒuːs/
tea *n****	/tiː/

Other words & phrases
excuse me	/ek'skjuːz miː/
hotel *n****	/həʊ'tel/
please***	/pliːz/
room *n****	/ruːm; rʊm/
thank you***	/θæŋk juː/

3A | Emergency workers

READING

1 Read about the people and match them to the photos.

1 This is Sylvie. She's from France. She's a doctor.

2 He's Edward and she's Francesca. They're from England. They're police officers.

3 My name's Frank. I'm from Germany. I'm an ambulance driver.

4 This is James. He's a firefighter. He's from New York.

5 I'm Giovanni and this is Sabrina. We're paramedics. We're from Italy.

2 Read the text again and complete the chart.

Name	Country	Job

VOCABULARY: jobs

1 🔘 **1.41** Listen and repeat the job words in the chart.

Language note

Use *a/an* with jobs.

2 Complete the sentences with *a/an*. What are these jobs in your language?

1 He's _____ teacher. 2 She's _____ student.
3 She's _____ doctor. 4 He's _____ actor.

3 🔘 **1.42** Listen and repeat.

C

PRONUNCIATION: /dʒ/, /d/, /r/ & /tʃ/

1 🔵 1.43 Listen and repeat the sounds and words.

/dʒ/   job
/d/   doctor
/r/   radio
/tʃ/   teacher

2 🔵 1.44 Listen and repeat the sentences.

1   The job is in Germany.
2   My teacher is from China.
3   David is a doctor from Denmark.
4   Ruslan is a taxi driver from Russia.

FUNCTIONAL LANGUAGE: asking about jobs

1 🔵 1.45 Read and listen. Say the phrases.

What's your job?
What do you do?
I'm a teacher.

2   Talk to five people in the class. Ask about their jobs.

GRAMMAR: *to be* (affirmative)

I *am* You *are* He/She/It *is*	*a student*	I'*m* You'*re* he'*s*/she'*s*/It'*s*	*a student*.
We *are* They *are*	*students.*	We'*re* They'*re*	*students.*

🔵 SEE LANGUAGE REFERENCE PAGE 40

1   Make the sentences with contractions.

1   I am a student.
    I'm a student.
2   We are from Spain.
3   He is an ambulance driver.
4   They are doctors.
5   She is from Chicago.
6   You are an actor.

2   Complete the sentences with *am/is/are*.

1   I _____ from Hong Kong.
2   My name _____ Yan Chee.
3   This _____ Mark.
4   He _____ an actor.
5   They _____ from Brazil.
6   You _____ a student.
7   We _____ firefighters.

SPEAKING

1   Work in pairs, A and B.

A: Turn to page 114.
B: Turn to page 118.
Complete the job files.

Useful language

His/her	name(s)	is ...
Their	phone number(s)	are ...

He/She	is	from ...
They	are	an actor/actors.
How do you spell that?		

3B | International train

VOCABULARY: colours and nationalities

1 🔘 **1.46** Listen and repeat the colours.

red   white   blue   black   yellow   green   brown

2 Match the country to the nationality.

1	France	a	Italian
2	Germany	b	French
3	Italy	c	Polish
4	Poland	d	Chinese
5	China	e	German
6	USA	f	American

3 🔘 **1.47** Listen to the recording to check your answers. Listen and repeat.

4 Describe the flags of the different countries.

The Italian flag is green, white and red.

5 What's your nationality? What colour is the flag of your country?

I'm Canadian. The Canadian flag is red and white.

LISTENING

1 🔘 **1.48** Listen to the conversation. What is the problem?

2 🔘 **1.48** Listen again and decide if the sentences are true (T) or false (F).

1 They are on a train.
2 The woman is from France.
3 The man is from the USA.
4 The train is the Spanish Express to Madrid.
5 The next stop is Milan.

GRAMMAR: *to be* (negative)

> To make the negative of *to be*, add *not* or *n't* to the verb.
> *I'm **not***
> *You **aren't***
> *He/She/It **isn't***   on the train.
> *We **aren't***
> *They **aren't***

 SEE LANGUAGE REFERENCE PAGE 40

1 🔘 1.49 Listen and correct the sentences.

1 Her name is Michelle. (Dominique)
   Her name isn't Michelle. Her name is Dominique.
2 She is from France. (Switzerland)
3 His name is Brad. (Mike)
4 He's Canadian. (American)
5 They're on a plane. (a train)
6 It's the Spanish Express. (Italian Express)

2 Complete the dialogues with the correct form of the verb *to be*.

1
A: This French wine (1) ____ (+) good.
B: It (2) ____ (-) French.
A: Excuse me?
B: It (3) ____ (-) French. It (4) ____ (+) Italian.
A: Really? Oh, yes, you (5) ____ (+) right. Italian white
   wine.

2
C: Where (6) ____ (+)
   you from in the United
   States?
D: We (7) ____ (-)
   American.
C: You (8) ____ (-)
   American?
D: No, we (9) ____ (+)
   from Canada.

3 🔘 1.50 Listen to the recording to check your answers.
Practise the dialogues.

PRONUNCIATION: contractions

1 🔘 1.51 Listen and tick (✔) the sentence you hear.

1
a) He is Scottish.
b) He's Scottish.

2
a) You are not David.
b) You're not David.

3
a) We are not Canadian.
b) We're not Canadian.

4
a) They are from France.
b) They're from France.

5
a) I am a student.
b) I'm a student.

6
a) I am not a teacher.
b) I'm not a teacher.

2 🔘 1.51 Listen again. Repeat the sentences.

SPEAKING

1 Read the sentences about famous people, things and
places. Which sentence is correct?

1 Volkswagen is from Germany.
2 Tokyo is in China.
3 Vladimir Putin is from Brazil.

2 Correct the incorrect sentences.

   Vladimir Putin isn't from Brazil. He's from Russia.

3 Make three similar sentences about people, places or
things: two incorrect and one correct.

4 Work in pairs, A and B.

A: Say your sentence.
B: Say *Correct!* or correct the incorrect sentence.

3c │ International school

READING

1 Look at the photos and answer the questions.

UNIS is the United Nations International School. It's in New York. At the United Nations International School there are teachers from 70 different countries and students from 115 different countries. UNIS is open six days a week, from Monday to Saturday.

1 What is UNIS?
2 Where is UNIS?

2 Read the text and check your answers.

VOCABULARY: days of the week

1 Complete the days of the week with a CAPITAL letter.

t	t	f	s	w	m	s

_onday   _uesday

_ednesday   _hursday

_riday   _aturday

_unday

2 🔘 1.52 Listen to the recording to check your answers. Repeat the days of the week.

LISTENING

1 🔘 1.53 Listen to a teacher from UNIS answer questions about the school. Number the questions in the correct order.

☐ Where are the teachers from?
☐ When is the school open?
☐ Is the school cafeteria open every day?
☐ Who is the Director?
☐ What is the school website?
☐ Are you the Director?

2 🔘 1.53 Listen again and match the answers to the questions.

☐ a Many teachers at UNIS are from the United States, but we also have French, German, Swiss, Italian, Japanese and Australian teachers.
☐ b No, it isn't. The cafeteria isn't open on Saturday.
☐ c It's www.unis.org.
☐ d No, I'm not. I'm the Assistant Director.
☐ e The director is Mr Wye. He's in his office right now.
☐ f The school is open Monday to Saturday.

GRAMMAR: verb *to be* (questions and short answers)

For *yes/no* questions, the subject and the verb change places.

> *The school **is** open.*
> ***Is** the school open?*

Short answers

> ***Are** you English?*
> **Yes**, I **am**./**No**, I'**m** not.

For *wh-* questions, put the question words: *what, when, who* and *where*, in front of the verb.

> ***Where** are you from?*
> ***When** is the school open?*

▷ SEE LANGUAGE REFERENCE PAGE 40

1 Complete the questions with the correct form of the verb *to be*.

1 What _____ your name?
2 Where _____ you from?
3 _____ you Spanish?
4 _____ it Monday today?
5 _____ your teacher British?

2 🔊 1.54 Listen to the recording to check your answers. Answer the questions.

3 Make questions with the words.

1 Where / the school?
2 / the school / open on Saturday?
3 When / the school /open?
4 Where / the teachers / from?
5 Who / the director?
6 / the director / from Vietnam?
7 Where / the director / from?

4 Work in pairs. Look at the information about the Hanoi UNIS. Ask and answer the questions in exercise 3.

UNIS Hanoi

United Nations International School in Hanoi, Vietnam

Open: Monday to Friday

Teachers from: Vietnam, United States, France, New Zealand, Australia, Spain, Canada, Finland

Director: Alun Cooper, England

FUNCTIONAL LANGUAGE: saying goodbye

1 🔊 1.55 Read and listen.

See you!
See you later.
See you on   Monday …   Tuesday …

2 Practise with other students.

ENGLISH AROUND YOU: the classroom

1 🔊 1.56 Read and listen to the phrases. Tick (✓) the ones you understand.

What's ___ in English?

How do you pronounce it?

How do you spell it?

Sorry, I don't understand.

2 Translate the phrases into your language.

3 What other English words or phrases are in the classroom?

3D | Review

READING & VOCABULARY

1 🔘 1.57 Read and listen to the text from the television guide. When are the Champions League matches? Complete with the correct day of the week.

Champions League football is back this week. Watch the best football teams in Europe in the quarter finals.

_____ matches

Chelsea (UK) V Barcelona (Spain)

Bayern Munich (Germany) V AC Milan (Italy)

_____ matches

Real Madrid (Spain) V Paris St Germain (France)

Lokomotiv Moscow (Russia) V Juventus (Italy)

2 Complete with the name of a team from the text.

1 The ____ colours are red and black.
2 ____ is a French team.
3 The ____ colours are black and white.
4 The ____ colours are blue and white.
5 ____ and ____ are Italian teams.
6 The ____ and ____ colours are blue and red.
7 The ____ colour is white.

GRAMMAR & VOCABULARY

1 Complete the sentences with the correct form of the verb *to be* and a job word from the box.

a teacher   actors   a firefighter
a taxi driver   students

1 They ____ ____.

2 She ____ ____.

3 They ____ ____.

4 She ____ ____.

5 He ____ ____.

2 🔘 1.58 Listen and check your answers. Say the sentences. Use contractions.

3 Cover the sentences in exercise 1. Work in pairs, A and B.

A: Say a sentence.
B: Point to the picture. Swap roles and repeat.

GRAMMAR

1 Match the questions and short answers.

1 Are you Italian?
2 Is he the teacher?
3 Are the police officers there?
4 Is she a doctor?
5 Is it Monday today?

a Yes, it is.
b Yes, they are.
c No, I'm not. I'm from Spain.
d No, she isn't. She's an ambulance driver.
e Yes, he is.

SPEAKING

1 Work in groups of three or four. Play the Q & A (Question and Answer) game. Your teacher will explain the rules.

Self assessment (tick ✓)
In English …
☐ I can say my job.
☐ I can say where I'm from.
☐ I can ask about jobs.

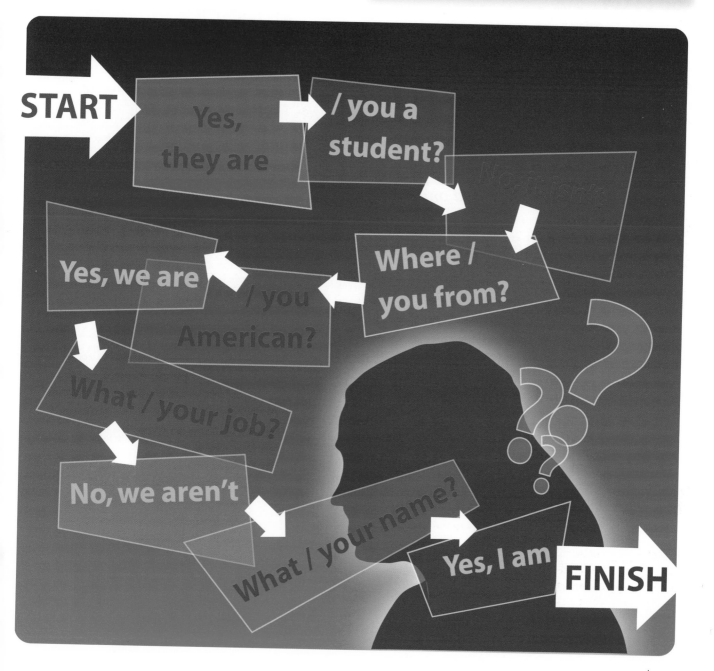

4A How old is it?

VOCABULARY: numbers 21–101

1 🔊 1.59 Listen and repeat.

20 twenty   30 thirty   70 seventy
40 forty   80 eighty
50 fifty   90 ninety
60 sixty   100 one hundred (a hundred)

2 🔊 1.60 Match the words to the numbers. Listen and repeat.

twenty-one   fifty-six
thirty-five   forty-two
seventy   sixty-three   eighty-eight
ninety-nine   one hundred and one

42   21   56   70   99
35   63   88   101

3 Work in pairs. Say three numbers to your partner. Your partner writes them down.

PRONUNCIATION: word stress (1)

1 🔊 1.61 Listen to the difference between these numbers.

☐ 13 thirteen   ☐ 30 thirty
☐ 14 fourteen   ☐ 40 forty
☐ 15 fifteen   ☐ 50 fifty

2 🔊 1.61 Listen again and repeat.

3 Say these numbers.

16 60   17 70
18 80   19 90

LISTENING

1 🔊 1.62 Listen to four conversations. Match each conversation to a picture.

A

B

C

D

2 🔘 **1.62** Listen again and complete the sentences.

1   The car is _____ years old.
2   The babies are _____ days old.
3   The computers are _____ years old.
4   The house is _____ years old.

Language note

There are
24 hours in a day.
7 days in a week.
4 weeks in a month.
12 months in a year.

FUNCTIONAL LANGUAGE: talking about age

1 🔘 **1.63** Read and listen.

How old is it?
It's five years old.
How old are you?
I'm thirty (years old).

2 🔘 **1.63** Listen again and repeat.

3   Look at the difference.

1 He's an old man.

He's a young man.

2 It's an old computer.

It's a new computer.

4 🔘 **1.64** Listen and repeat the sentences.

GRAMMAR: *it, they*

Use *it* for things.
   The house is seventy years old.
   It's seventy years old.
Use *they* for people or things.
   The computers are two years old.
   They're two years old.
   The babies are thirteen months old.
   They're thirteen months old.

🔘 SEE LANGUAGE REFERENCE PAGE 40

1   Read the texts and replace the underlined word(s) with *he, she, it* or *they*.

1   The house is in Switzerland. The house is in Geneva. The house isn't new. The house is one hundred and twenty years old.
2   These mobile phones are from Japan. The mobile phones are new. The mobile phones are only six months old.
3   This is Mark and Sylvia. Mark and Sylvia are French students. Sylvia is from England and Mark is from Scotland. This is their school. Their school is in Paris. Their school is fifteen years old.

2 🔘 **1.65** Listen to the recording to check your answers. Say the texts.

SPEAKING

1   Work in pairs. Ask each other questions with *How old ...?*

   How old is your ...?

Useful language

Sorry, I don't have one.
I don't know.
I think he's forty years old.
She's young/old.
It's new/old.

4B | Family album

READING

1 Look at the family album webpage. Where is the family from?

www.TheMurphyFamily.com

Home   Photo Archive   Special Events   Updates   Message Boards   Email

Michael and Jennifer Murphy's Family album.

This is our new baby, Sean. He's sixteen months old now!

My wife's parents: Donna and Martin. They are from Oxford. They're teachers.

This is my grandparents' house in Cork, Ireland. The house is two hundred years old.

This is my sister, Sharon with her friend, Diane. Diane's American. She's an actor.

2 Read the text again and answer the questions.

1 How old is Sean?
2 Where is the grandparents' house?
3 Where is Diana from?
4 What is Diana's job?
5 Where are Donna and Martin from?
6 What is their job?

VOCABULARY: family

1 🔊 1.66 Listen and repeat the family words. What are they in your language?

1 a husband and wife
2 a father, mother and their son and daughter
3 a mother and her children
4 grandparents, parents and children

2 Put the words from exercise 1 in the correct categories.

3 Put these words in the correct column in exercise 2. What are the family words in your language?

| grandmother | grandfather | brother | sister |

4 Work in pairs. Answer the questions.

1 Which of the families in exercise 1 is more common in your country?
2 How old are people in your country when they:
   a) get married?
   b) have a child?
   c) have grandchildren?

PRONUNCIATION /ə/

1 🔘 1.67 Listen how the underlined sound is pronounced in these words.

| fath<u>er</u>   moth<u>er</u>   daught<u>er</u>   act<u>or</u> |
| umbrell<u>a</u>   doct<u>or</u> |

2 🔘 1.68 Listen and repeat the sentences. Pronounce the underlined sounds as /ə/.

1 My fath<u>er</u> is <u>a</u>n act<u>or</u>.
2 My moth<u>er</u> is from <u>A</u>meric<u>a</u>. She's <u>A</u>meric<u>a</u>n.
3 On S<u>a</u>tur<u>d</u>ay, I'm with my grandpar<u>e</u>nts.

GRAMMAR: possessive 's

Use 's to show possession.
   My wife's parents.

If the word ends in *s*, put the ' after the *s*.
   My grandparents' house.

🔘 SEE LANGUAGE REFERENCE PAGE 40

1 Find all the examples of 's in the text on page 34. Decide if they are possessive 's or contraction 's.

2 Complete the sentences about the Murphy family.

1 Donna is Jennifer's ____.
2 Michael is Jennifer's ____.
3 Michael is Sharon's ____.
4 Sean is Michael and Jennifer's ____.
5 Jennifer is Martin's ____.

3 Make other sentences about the Murphys. Use the possessive.

   Sean ⟶ Michael.
   Sean is Michael's son.
1 Sean ⟶ Jennifer.
2 Jennifer ⟶ Michael
3 Donna and Martin ⟶ Jennifer.
4 Martin ⟶ Sean.

SPEAKING

1 Write the names of three people from your family on a piece of paper.

2 Prepare a short presentation about these people. Use the ideas for what to say.

   This is …   *They are my …*
   His name is …   *He's a …*
   She's from …   *He's … years old.*

3 When you are ready, tell a partner about the people.

ENGLISH AROUND YOU: family words

1 🔘 1.69 Read and listen to these different informal family words. What do they mean?

kids   gran   grandad   mum   dad

4c | Where's my black bag?

VOCABULARY: personal possessions

1 🔘 1.70 Look at the pictures and listen to the words.

glasses   sunglasses   a jacket   a wallet   a bag   keys

an MP3 player   a mobile phone   a photograph   an ID card   money   an umbrella

2 🔘 1.70 Listen again and repeat the words.

3 What is in your bag today? Tell a partner.

keys, photographs, a wallet …

LISTENING

1 🔘 1.71 Mark and Lee are housemates. Listen to three short conversations. What does Lee want in each conversation?

1 _____

2 _____

3 _____

2 🔘 1.71 Listen again. Match the words in the box to the letters A–C on the picture. There are two extra words.

glasses   bag   keys   wallet   money

GRAMMAR: prepositions of place

In, on, under, next to, behind and in front of are prepositions of place.
Put them before the noun.
*It's **on** the table*
*Is it **under** the table?*
*It isn't **in** my bag.*
*It's **next to** you.*

> SEE LANGUAGE REFERENCE PAGE 40

1 Where are Lee's things? Make sentences. Read the tapescript on page 121 to check your answers.

2 Rearrange the words to make sentences.

1 jacket   the   The   on   table   is.
2 book   glasses   The   are   on   the
3 the   table   under   are   The   keys
4 The   door   the   front   in   table   is   of
5 sandwich   The   under   the   newspapers   is

3 Make sentences. Use the words and a preposition of place.

1 The man / the table.

2 The dog / the bath.

3 It / you!

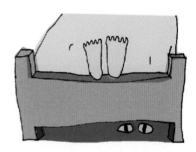

4 The cat / the bed.

5 John / George.

6 The woman / the boy.

SPEAKING

1 Work in pairs, A and B.

A: Turn to page 115.
B: Turn to page 117.

Describe and draw your pictures.

U.S. Politics –

It's a family affair

Bill Clinton

Hillary Clinton

George Bush

Jeb Bush

George W. Bush

LISTENING

1 What do you know about the people in the pictures? Make sentences.

George W. Bush is George Bush's son.

2 🔊 1.72 Listen to the recording to check your answers.

3 🔊 1.72 Listen again and complete the sentences with a word from the box. There are three extra words.

brothers   wife   father   brother
sister   husband

1 Hillary Clinton is Bill Clinton's ____.
2 George Bush is George W. Bush's ____.
3 Jeb Bush and George W. Bush are ____.

VOCABULARY

1 Complete the sentences so they are true for you.

1 My family is from …
2 My father's name is …
3 My mother's name is …
4 (I am/I'm not) married.

2 Work with a partner. Compare your sentences.

3 Make words from the cards.

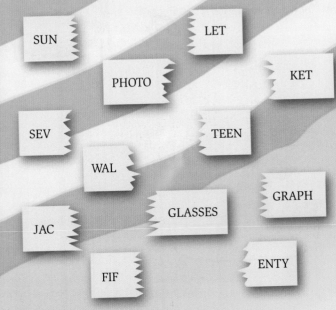

SUN   LET   PHOTO   KET   SEV   TEEN   WAL   GRAPH   GLASSES   JAC   ENTY   FIF

FUNCTIONAL LANGUAGE

1 Complete the sentences with a word or letters.

1 How *old* is **it**?
   It's ten years old.
2 How old are you?
   She's twenty-nine and I'm twenty-four years ____.
3 Is he eighteen ____ old?
   No, **he** isn't. He's sixteen.
4 How old are **they**?
   They'____ seven weeks old.
5 How old is **she**?
   She'____ ninety-five years old.

2 Think of a word or words to replace the words in bold in exercise 3.

   How old is your car?
   It's ten years old.

GRAMMAR

1 There are five grammatical mistakes in this text. Correct the mistakes.

This is my sister, Lisa. Lisa is a architect. Lisa husband is a teacher. His name are James. They Canadian. James is from Toronto and Lisa's is from Montreal.

2 Make a similar text about two people in your family.

   This is …

SPEAKING

1 Work in pairs. Look at the picture. Ask and answer questions about the objects.

   Where's the computer?
   It's on the table.

Self assessment (tick ✓)
In English …
☐ I can count to 100.
☐ I can talk about age.
☐ I can talk about my family.
☐ I can say where things are in relation to other things.

GRAMMAR

Verb *to be*: present simple

Affirmative				
Full form			**Contraction**	
I	am		I'm	
He/She/It	is	from Canada.	He's/She's/It's	fine.
You/We/They	are		You're/We're/They're	

To make the verb *to be* negative, add *not* (or *n't*) to the verb.

Negative	
Full form	**Contraction**
I am not from Spain.	I'm not from Spain.
He/She/It is not a teacher.	He/She/It isn't a teacher.
You/We/They are not in class.	You/We/They aren't in class. or You're/We're/They're not in class.

To make questions with the verb *to be,* put the verb before the subject.

verb	**subject**
Are	*you married?*

Question		
Am	I	
Is	he/she/it	30 years old?
Are	you/we/they	

Short answer		
	I	am 'm not.
Yes, No,	he/she/it	is. isn't.
	you/we/they	are. aren't.

It, they

It and *they* are pronouns.
Use *it* for things.
> The house is in London. **It** is in London.

Use *they* for people or things.
> The houses are in London. **They** are in London.
> Philip and Katy are English. **They** are English.

Possessive *'s*

Use *'s* to show possession.
> John**'s** mother.
> My sister**'s** friend.

If the word ends in an *-s*, add ':
> His parents' house.
> Not ~~The house of his parents.~~
> The babies' rooms.
> Not ~~The room of the babies.~~

Prepositions

in

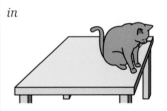

on

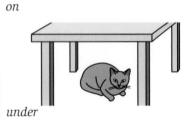

under

next to

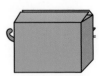

behind

in front of

FUNCTIONAL LANGUAGE

Asking about jobs
What's your job?
What do you do?
I'm a/an … .

Saying goodbye
See you!
See you later.
See you on
   Monday ….
   Tuesday ….

Talking about age
How old is it?
It's five years old.

How old are you?
I'm thirty (years old).

WORD LIST

Jobs
actor *n****	/'æktə/
architect *n*	/ɑːkɪtekt/
doctor *n****	/'dɒktə/
driver *n****	/'draɪvə/
firefighter *n*	/'faɪəˌfaɪtə/
paramedic *n*	/ˌpærə'medɪk/
police officer *n*	/pə'liːs ˌɒfɪsə/
student *n****	/'stjuːdənt/
teacher *n****	/'tiːtʃə/

Colours
black *adj****	/blæk/
blue *adj****	/bluː/
brown *adj****	/braʊn/
green *adj****	/griːn/
red *adj****	/red/
white *adj****	/waɪt/
yellow *adj****	/'jeləʊ/

Days of the week
Saturday *n****	/'sætədi/
Sunday *n****	/'sʌndi/
Monday *n****	/'mʌndi/
Tuesday *n****	/'tjuːzdi/
Wednesday *n****	/'wenzdi/
Thursday *n****	/'θɜːzdi/
Friday *n****	/'fraɪdi/

Nationalities
American *adj*	/ə'merɪkən/
Chinese *adj*	/tʃaɪ'niːz/
French *adj*	/frentʃ/
German *adj*	/'dʒɜːmən/
Italian *adj*	/ɪ'tæljən/
Polish *adj*	/'pəʊlɪʃ/

Family words
brother *n****	/'brʌðə/
child *n****	/tʃaɪld/
daughter *n****	/'dɔːtə/
father *n****	/'fɑːðə/
grandfather *n**	/'grænˌfɑːðə/
grandmother *n**	/'grænˌmʌðə/
grandparents *n**	/'grænˌpeərənts/
husband *n****	/'hʌzbənd/
mother *n****	/'mʌðə/
parents *n****	/'peərənts/
sister *n****	/'sɪstə/
son *n****	/sʌn/
wife *n****	/waɪf/

Personal possessions
bag *n****	/bæg/
glasses *n*	/'glɑːsɪz/
ID card *n*	/aɪ'diː ˌkɑːd/
jacket *n***	/'dʒækət/
keys *n****	/kiːz/
mobile phone *n*	/ˌməʊbaɪl 'fəʊn/
money *n****	/'mʌni/
MP3 player *n*	/empiː'θriː ˌpleɪə/
photograph *n****	/'fəʊtəˌgrɑːf/
sunglasses *n*	/'sʌnˌglɑːsɪz/
umbrella *n*	/ʌm'brelə/
wallet *n*	/'wɒlət/

Other words & phrases
ambulance *n**	/'æmbjələns/
baby *n****	/'beɪbɪ/
car *n****	/kɑː/
correct *adj****	/kə'rekt/
flag *n*	/flæg/
house *n****	/haʊs/
international *adj****	/ɪntə'næʃnəl/
new *adj****	/njuː/
old *adj****	/əʊld/
train *n****	/treɪn/
wine *n****	/waɪn/
young *adj****	/jʌŋ/

5A │ World of work

VOCABULARY: common verbs and nouns (1)

1 🔘 1.73 Look at the picture. Listen and repeat the sentences.

I live in New York.
I work for a big company.
I go to work by taxi.

2 Complete the tables with the words in the box.

| a house   an office   car |

	for	a big company.
I work	in	a factory. a shop.

	in	New York. ——— a flat.
I live	with	my parents. my boyfriend. my wife and children.
	alone.	

			by	train. bus.
I go	to school/ to work		on	foot.

3 Make three sentences about you. Use the phrases from exercise 2.

READING

1 Read the texts. Match the texts 1–3 to the pictures A–C.

1
Keith Wright lives in London. He's an actor and he works in a restaurant. He goes to work by train. Keith lives in a flat. He lives with two other actors.

2
Tom and Christine are American. They live in Mexico. They're teachers and they work at the University of Oaxaca. Their house is in a small town. The town is next to Oaxaca and they go to work by bus.

3
Charri is from the Philippines. She lives in Manila. She lives with her grandparents, her parents, her husband and children. She works in a factory. Every day, Charri goes to work on foot. The factory is two hours from her house.

2 Read the texts again. Who is speaking? Write C (Charri), B (Bob) or TC (Tom and Christine).

1 ☐ We're teachers.
2 ☐ I work in a factory.
3 ☐ I go to work by train.
4 ☐ I live in London.
5 ☐ We live next to Oaxaca.
6 ☐ I go to work on foot.

GRAMMAR: present simple (1) (affirmative)

Use the present simple to talk about things that are true.
They live in Mexico.
She works in a factory.
I go to work by car.
We live in Mexico.

▶ SEE LANGUAGE REFERENCE PAGE 58

1 Find all examples of the verbs *go, live* and *work* in the text. Complete the rule.

After *he, she* or *it*, add _____ to the verb in the present simple.

2 Choose the correct option, a or b.

1
a) I work in London.
b) I works in London.

2
a) They lives in Japan.
b) They live in Japan.

3
a) He works in a car factory.
b) He work in a car factory.

4
a) We live with our parents.
b) We lives with our parents.

5
a) Vanessa goes to school by bus.
b) Vanessa go to school by bus.

3 Complete the text with a verb from the box in the correct form.

live (x2)   work (x2)   go (x1)

I (1) _____ with my brother Josh. We (2) _____ in a house. The house is in the centre of San Francisco. I (3) _____ in an office. Josh is a shop assistant. He (4) _____ in a bookshop. The bookshop and the office are in the centre of San Francisco. We (5) _____ to work on foot.

SPEAKING

1 Prepare a short text about you. Use the texts in Reading exercise 1 to help you.

2 Work in pairs. Tell your partner about you.

3 Work with a new student. Talk about your partner.

He/she lives in …
He/she lives with …
He/she works in …

5B | Technology and you

VOCABULARY: technology

1 Match the words 1–7 to the pictures A–G.

1 a computer
2 an email address
3 a website
4 a fax machine
5 a mobile phone
6 a printer
7 a digital camera

2 🔊 1.74 Listen and repeat the words.

3 Do you have these things at work, at school or at home? Tell a partner.

We have computers at work.
I have a digital camera at home.

> ### Language note: *have*
>
> The present simple of *have* has two forms, *have* and *has*.
> *I, you, we, they* **have**
> *He, she, it* **has**

FUNCTIONAL LANGUAGE: emails

1 🔊 1.75 Listen and repeat how we say these words and symbols in English.

@ at   • dot   / slash   **com** com

2 🔊 1.76 Listen and repeat the conversation.

What's your email address?
It's veronica@hotmail.com

3 What's your email address? Ask three people in the class.

What's your email address?
It's …
Sorry, I don't have one.

LISTENING

1 🔊 1.77 Listen to people talk about technology and their work. Tick (✓) the words you hear.

computer   mobile phone   website   email
office   digital camera   car

2 🔊 1.77 Listen again and decide if the sentences are true (T) or false (F).

Conversation 1
1 The woman writes personal emails at work.
2 The man has a mobile phone.

Conversation 2
3 The woman has one computer at work.
4 The man and woman don't have a computer at home.

Conversation 3
5 The machine is a fax machine.
6 The woman doesn't use the fax machine.

GRAMMAR: present simple (2) (negative; *and* + *but*)

> Use *don't/doesn't* to make the negative in the present simple.
> **I don't** have an email address.
> She **doesn't** have a computer at home.
> Use *and* or *but* to link words or phrases.
> *And* gives more information.
> I have a computer **and** I use it.
> *But* shows a contrast
> We have a fax machine, **but** we don't use it.

> SEE LANGUAGE REFERENCE PAGE 58

1 Complete the sentences with the verb in the correct form.

1 I ____ (not write) personal emails.
2 I ____ (not know) anything about computers or technology.
3 We ____ (use) the computers a lot. We ____ (have) a fax machine, but we ____ (not use) it. Everything is email now.

2 Tick (✓) the sentences that are true for your teacher. Change the sentences that aren't true.

1 The teacher has a computer.
2 He/She has an email address.
3 He/She goes to work by bus.
4 He/She lives next to the school.
5 He/She has three brothers and sisters.

3 Complete the sentences with *and* or *but*.

1 She lives in Spain ____ she works in Spain.
2 She lives in Spain ____ she works in France.
3 He has a computer at work ____ he has a computer at home.
4 He has a computer at work ____ he doesn't have a computer at home.

PRONUNCIATION: /s/ & /z/

1 🔘 1.78 Listen and repeat the sounds and words.

/s/	/z/
works	has
seven	Brazil
desk	please
Spain	does

2 🔘 1.79 Listen and repeat the sentences.

1 The student's name is Samantha.
2 She works in Spain.
3 She has two mobile phones.
4 She doesn't use computers.

SPEAKING

1 Read the *Technology and you* survey. Put a tick (✓) or a cross (✗) in the boxes.

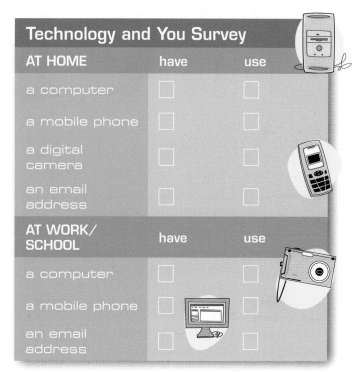

Technology and You Survey		
AT HOME	have	use
a computer	☐	☐
a mobile phone	☐	☐
a digital camera	☐	☐
an email address	☐	☐
AT WORK/ SCHOOL	have	use
a computer	☐	☐
a mobile phone	☐	☐
an email address	☐	☐

2 Work in pairs. Tell your partner about technology and you.

I have a computer at home and at work.
I use a computer at work but I don't use a computer at home.

ENGLISH AROUND YOU: computers

1 Many computer words are English. Tick (✓) the words you know. What are these words in your language?

> Windows   a mouse   World Wide Web   Word Explorer   save   cancel

2 🔘 1.80 Listen and repeat the words in exercise 1.

3 What other computer words do you know in English?

5c | New job

READING & LISTENING

1 Look at the picture of Lord Duncan. What does he do?

2 🔘 1.81 Read and listen to the interview with Lord Duncan about his new job. Is it a difficult job?

Interviewer:	Lord Duncan, nice to meet you. You are the new president of Duncan Enterprises. Tell us about your new job.
Lord Duncan:	It's an interesting job, but it isn't easy.
Interviewer:	Really?
Lord Duncan:	Well, I have my father's job. I work a lot.
Interviewer:	Do you work every day?
Lord Duncan:	No, I don't. Not every day. I work from Monday to Wednesday.
Interviewer:	Do you work in your father's old office?
Lord Duncan:	No, I don't. I have my own offices now.
Interviewer:	Offices? Do you have more than one office?
Lord Duncan:	Yes, I do. I have two offices. One for me and one for the two secretaries.
Interviewer:	I see. Two secretaries. Do they work Monday to Wednesday?
Lord Duncan:	No, no, no. No, they don't. They work Monday to Saturday.
Interviewer:	Ah.
Lord Duncan:	I have a game of golf today. Do you have any other questions?
Interviewer:	No, I don't. Thank you, Lord Duncan.
Lord Duncan:	You're welcome.

3 Read the interview again and choose the correct answer.

1 Lord Duncan is the _____ of Duncan Enterprises.
   a) secretary
   b) student
   c) President
2 He works _____ a week.
   a) five days
   b) two days
   c) three days
3 Lord Duncan's father _____ in the company.
   a) lives
   b) doesn't work
   c) works
4 Lord Duncan has _____
   a) two offices and two secretaries.
   b) two offices and a secretary.
   c) an office and two secretaries.

VOCABULARY: adjectives (1)

1 🔘 1.82 Listen and repeat the sentences.

It's a difficult job.
It's a boring job.
It's a good job.

2 Match the words in the box to their opposites in exercise 1.

bad   interesting   easy

3 Work in pairs. Make sentences about these jobs. Use the adjectives from exercises 1 and 2.

1 Lord Duncan's job
1 *Lord Duncan has an easy job.*
2 the President of your country
3 a teacher
4 a university student
5 a police officer

Language note

Adjectives can come in two places in a sentence.
- before a noun   *a good day*
- after the verb *to be*   *It's good.*

GRAMMAR: present simple (3) (questions and short answers)

To make questions in the present simple, use the auxiliary verb *do* + subject + infinitive.

Do you work *every day?*

If the subject is *he/she/it*, use *does* + subject + infinitive.

Does your father work *in the company?*

Short answers
Yes + subject + *do/does.*
No + subject + *don't/doesn't*
    Yes, I do.
    No he doesn't.

> SEE LANGUAGE REFERENCE PAGE 58

1 Make questions and answers about Lord Duncan.

1 he / work on Monday?   ✓
Does he work on Monday? Yes, he does.
2 he / go to work by bus?   ✗
3 he / live next to the office?   ✓
4 he / have two secretaries?   ✓
5 he / work on Saturday?   ✗
6 he / have an easy job?   ✓

2 Rearrange the words to make questions.

1 to   school   go   you   Do   bus   by?
2 in   work   an   office   you   Do?
3 a   car   you   Do   have?
4 Saturday   on   work   you   Do?

3 Work in pairs. Ask and answer the questions in exercise 2.

PRONUNCIATION: intonation (2)

1 🔘 1.83 Listen to the intonation in these questions.

Does he have a job?

Do you use a computer?

Are you a student?

2 🔘 1.83 Listen again and repeat the questions. Copy the intonation.

SPEAKING

1 Play *My new job*. Work in pairs, A and B.

A: You have a new job. Choose one of the jobs in the picture. Don't tell B. Answer B's questions.
B: Ask questions about A's new job. Use the words below to help you. Guess A's new job.

DO YOU …
… have   a difficult job?
                an easy job?
                a good job?
… use   a computer?
… work   with other people?
                alone?
                Monday to Friday?
… work in   a hospital?
                a school?
                an office?
ARE YOU A/AN …?

2 Swap roles and repeat the activity.

5D | Review

READING

1 Work in two groups, A and B.

1 Group A read about Milo.
2 Group B read about Bertie.

It's a dog's life

MILO

Milo is from America, but he lives in London. He goes to work Monday to Saturday. Milo works with the police. He is a police dog. He works in different places: at the airport, at schools and on the streets. Milo's partner is Officer Simon Pott. Simon and Milo work together and they live together. They're good friends.

2 Answer the questions about the dog in your text.

1 Where is he from?
2 Where does he live?
3 Does he work every day?
4 Does he live alone?
5 Where does he work?
6 Does he have a difficult life?

3 Work with a partner from the other group. Compare your answers about the different dogs.

BERTIE

Bertie is an English dog, but he doesn't live in England. He lives in Paris with his owner, Eugenie. Eugenie works for a French fashion magazine. Bertie doesn't work every day. He is a show dog and he goes to dog shows. The dog shows are in hotels in different cities: London, Madrid, Milan. When Bertie has a dog show, he and Eugenie go to the best hotel in town.

GRAMMAR

1 Make questions with the words.

1 Milo / a police dog? *Is Milo a police dog?*
2 Milo / English?
3 Milo / work at the airport?
4 Simon and Milo / work together?
5 Simon and Milo / live in America?
6 Simon / live with Milo?
7 Bertie / an English dog?
8 Bertie / work in England?
9 Eugenie / work for an English magazine?
10 Bertie and Eugenie / live in Paris?

2 Work in pairs. Ask and answer the questions. Use the information in the Reading.

1 *Is Milo a police dog? Yes, he is.*

VOCABULARY

1 Find six technology words in the wordsearch.

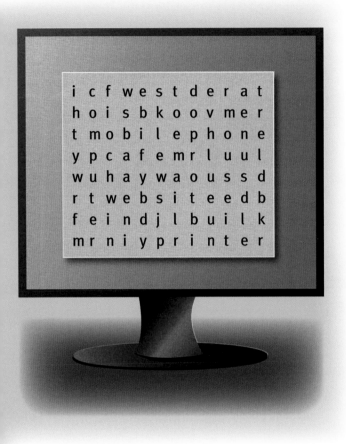

```
i c f w e s t d e r a t
h o i s b k o o v m e r
t m o b i l e p h o n e
y p c a f e m r l u u l
w u h a y w a o u s s d
r t w e b s i t e e d b
f e i n d j l b u i l k
m r n i y p r i n t e r
```

2 Match the symbol to the word.

1 @   a email address
2 .   b at
3 /   c dot
4 jim@aol.com d slash

3 🔘 1.84 Listen and circle the email address you hear. Repeat the emails.

1 hal006@mail.com   hel06@mail.com
2 sofia@ya.net   sofia@ia.net
3 mercedes@car.com   mercedes@kar.com

FUNCTIONAL LANGUAGE

1 Work in pairs, A and B. You are going to practise saying email addresses and website URLs.

A: Turn to page 116.
B: Turn to page 114.

2 Do you know any other URLs? What are they? Tell a partner.

SPEAKING

1 Work in small groups. Make questions with the information in the box.

Do you	have		a dog? an email address?
	work/ live		in a house? in a flat? next to the school?
	go	(to work) (to school)	by car? by bus?

2 Tell the class three things about the group.

Pablo and Diana live in a house.
Ana goes to work by car, but Ivan goes to work by bus.

Self assessment (tick ✓)
In English ...
☐ I can say where I live and work.
☐ I can say email addresses.
☐ I can say websites.

6A | Night and day

VOCABULARY: common verbs and nouns (2)

1 🔊 **1.85** Match the verbs and phrases to the pictures. Listen and repeat the verbs.

> eat   drink   go to bed   wake up
> read   sleep

A

B

C

D

E

F

2 Complete the space with a verb from exercise 1.

_____ a sandwich/an apple/breakfast
_____ water/coffee/tea
_____ a newspaper/a book/a magazine

3 Put the verb phrases in order to make a typical Monday morning for you.

go to work/school
drink coffee/tea/juice/milk
wake up
eat breakfast

On Monday morning I wake up, eat breakfast …

Mornings are different for different people. For some people, mornings are always easy. They always wake up early. They eat breakfast, they read the morning newspaper and they go to work on time. These are morning people.

For other people, mornings are often very difficult. They always go to bed late at night. They sleep late and they wake up late. They sometimes drink a cup of coffee but they don't often eat breakfast (because they are usually late for work). These are night people.

You don't decide to be a morning person or a night person. It's genetic.

Glossary
on time = not late

READING

1 Read the article. What is it about?

1 A typical morning
2 Morning people and night people
3 When people sleep

Language note

person (singular)   *people* (plural)

2 Read again and decide if the sentences are about morning people (☀) or night people (☾).

1 ☀ ☾   Mornings are easy.

2 ☀ ☾   They go to bed late at night.

3 ☀ ☾   They read the morning newspaper.

4 ☀ ☾   They eat breakfast.

5 ☀ ☾   Mornings are difficult.

6 ☀ ☾   They don't eat breakfast.

3 Are you a morning person or a night person? Tell a partner.

GRAMMAR: adverbs of frequency

always   often/usually   sometimes   hardly ever   never

Use adverbs of frequency to say how often we do something.
   They **always** *go to bed late at night.*
Adverbs of frequency go before the main verb.
   They **sometimes** *drink a cup of coffee.*
   They *don't* **often** *eat breakfast.*
Adverbs of frequency go after the verb *to be*.
   Mornings are **often** *very difficult.*

❯ SEE LANGUAGE REFERENCE PAGE 58

1   Rewrite the sentence with the word in brackets.

1   Mike works on Saturday morning. (always)
2   He goes to bed late on Friday night. (sometimes)
3   He hears the alarm clock. (hardly ever)
4   He is tired. (always)
5   He eats a big breakfast. (usually)
6   He is late for work. (often)

2   🔘 1.86 Listen and check your answers. Repeat the sentences.

3   Change the sentences in exercise 1 so they are true for you.

PRONUNCIATION: /e/, /ʌ/, /uː/ & /ɪ/

1   🔘 1.87 Listen and repeat the sounds and words

/e/ never, bed
/ʌ/ sometimes, up
/uː/ juice, usually
/ɪ/ difficult, it

2   🔘 1.88 Listen and repeat the sentences.

1   It's a typical morning for Lynne.
2   She usually has juice.
3   Her friend Ed is still in bed.
4   Ed never gets up early.
5   On Sundays, he sometimes doesn't wake up before one.

FUNCTIONAL LANGUAGE: telling the time (1)

1   🔘 1.89 Listen and repeat the dialogue.

A: What time is it?
B: It's eight thirty.

Language note

am/pm
am = *in the morning*
pm = *in the afternoon/evening*

❯ SEE LANGUAGE REFERENCE PAGE 58

2   🔘 1.90 Listen and circle the times you hear.

1   8.15pm / 8.50pm
2   7 o'clock in the morning / 7 o'clock in the evening
3   9.20am / 9.20pm
4   12.35 / 12.25

3   What time is it? Work in pairs. Ask and answer the question with these times.

10.00am   1.25pm   12.15am
12.50am   4.00pm   3.45pm

SPEAKING

1   Complete the sentences so they are true for you.

On Monday I usually wake up at …
On Sunday I usually wake up at …
I *use/don't use* an alarm clock.
I *usually/sometimes/never* watch TV late at night.
I am *usually/sometimes/always* tired at 11.00pm.
I usually go to bed at …

2   Work in pairs. Tell your partner about you.

3   Change pairs and repeat the exercise.

6B | Free time

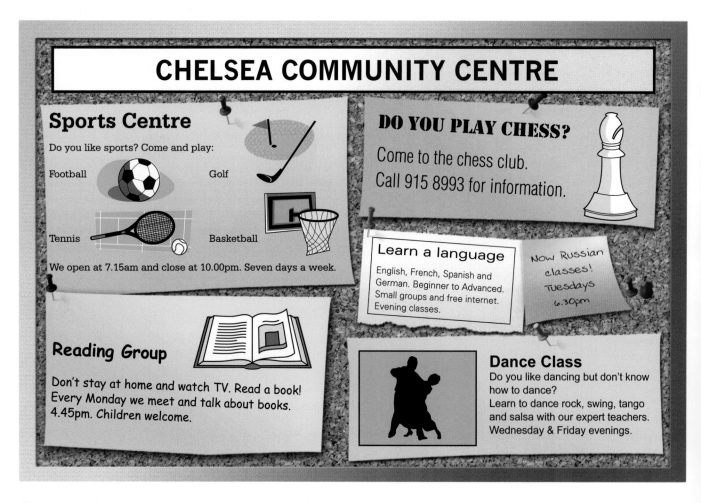

CHELSEA COMMUNITY CENTRE

Sports Centre

Do you like sports? Come and play:

Football   Golf

Tennis   Basketball

We open at 7.15am and close at 10.00pm. Seven days a week.

DO YOU PLAY CHESS?

Come to the chess club.
Call 915 8993 for information.

Learn a language

English, French, Spanish and German. Beginner to Advanced. Small groups and free internet. Evening classes.

Now Russian classes! Tuesdays 6.30pm

Reading Group

Don't stay at home and watch TV. Read a book! Every Monday we meet and talk about books. 4.45pm. Children welcome.

Dance Class

Do you like dancing but don't know how to dance?
Learn to dance rock, swing, tango and salsa with our expert teachers. Wednesday & Friday evenings.

READING & VOCABULARY: common verbs and nouns (3), free time activities

1 Read the different notices. <u>Underline</u> the verbs. What are these verbs in your language?

2 Complete the sentences with a verb from exercise 1.

1 On Saturday mornings I ____ football in the park.
2 I don't ____ chess.
3 Many people in my country ____ English at evening classes.
4 I ____ TV at night.
5 I know how to ____ salsa.
6 I ____ sports.

3 🔘 1.91 Listen to the recording to check your answers.

4 Make the sentences in exercise 2 true for you.

LISTENING

1 🔘 1.92 Listen to a person phone the Chelsea Community Centre. Tick (✔) the free time activities she asks about.

1 chess
2 golf
3 reading
4 language class
5 dance class

2 🔘 1.92 Listen again. <u>Underline</u> the correct answer.

1 The *chess club / dance class* meets on Saturdays.
2 It's at 10 o'clock *in the morning / at night*.
3 It's *8 pounds / 5 pounds* for the month.
4 The language school phone number is *9013 / 9023*.

Language note

£1 (pound) = 100 pence (p)

GRAMMAR: present simple (4) (*wh*- questions)

Who, what, where, when and *how* are question words. Put them in front of the auxiliary verb.
What *do you do in your free time?*
When *do you play football?*

> SEE LANGUAGE REFERENCE PAGE 58

1 Read the dialogue and complete with the words in the box.

how much	when	where	who	what

A: (1) _____ do you do after work?
B: I have a Russian class.
A: Really? (2) _____ do you learn Russian?
B: At the community centre.
A: (3) _____ is the class?
B: 6.30pm.
A: (4) _____ do you go with?
B: My friend Mike.
A: (5) _____ does it cost?
B: It's free.

2 🔊 1.93 Listen to the recording to check your answers. Work in pairs. Read the dialogue.

3 Make questions.

1 when / you have free time?
   When do you have free time?
2 where / you live?
3 where/ you work?
4 what / you do in your free time?
5 where / you go in your free time?

PRONUNCIATION: connected speech (1)

1 🔊 1.94 Listen to the questions from Grammar exercise 3. Notice how some words are linked together.

When do you have free time?

2 🔊 1.95 Listen and repeat.

free time
have free time
you have free time
do you have free time
When do you have free time?

3 Repeat with the other questions from Grammar exercise 3.

4 Work in pairs. Ask and answer the questions.

When do you have free time?
On Saturday and Sunday.

FUNCTIONAL LANGUAGE: telling the time (2)

1 🔊 1.96 Listen and repeat the times.

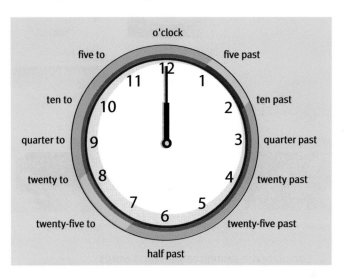

Language note

at + times (*at six o'clock, at half past two*)

2 🔊 1.97 Listen and repeat the dialogue.

A: What time is the English class?
B: It's at a quarter past six.

3 Work in pairs. Make other questions about the activities on page 52.

What time is …?
It's at …

SPEAKING

1 Work in pairs, A and B.

A: You are a famous person (you decide who).
B: Interview A. Use the questions in Grammar exercise 3.

2 Swap roles and repeat.

6c | Eating habits

VOCABULARY & SPEAKING: food (2) and meals

1 🔘 2.1 Listen and repeat the food words.

eggs   toast   fruit

milk   soup   chicken

meat   fish   pasta

salad   ice cream   vegetables

2 Complete the sentences with food words.

1 I often have ____ for breakfast.
2 I usually have ____ for lunch.
3 I never have ____ for dinner.
4 I like ____ but I don't like ____.

Language note

With food and drink we can use the verb *have*.
Have = *eat* or *drink*.
   I have coffee. = *I drink coffee.*
   I have fish. = *I eat fish.*

3 Make questions with the words.

1 What time / have breakfast?
2 What / have for breakfast?
3 What time / have lunch?
4 What / have for lunch?
5 What time / have dinner?
6 What / have for dinner?

4 Work in pairs. Ask and answer the questions in exercise 3.

READING & LISTENING

1 Look at the Eating Habits survey. It's difficult to see some of the words. What words are missing?

Eating Habits Survey

1 Do you have three meals a d _____ ?
   ☐ YES   ☐ NO

2 Do you e _____ fruit and/or vegetables every day?
   ☐ YES   ☐ NO

3 Do you eat meat and/or f _____ every day?
   ☐ YES   ☐ NO

4 How often do you have a meal at a rest _____ ?
   _____

5 How often do you eat with your fam _____ ?
   _____

6 How often do you have lunch at work/sc _____ ?
   _____

2 🔘 2.2 Listen to the recording to check your answers.

3 🔘 2.2 Listen to the recording again and match the answers to the questions.

a Well … I eat at home on Friday, but the other days I eat at work. So four times a week.
b We have dinner together every night.
c Do you mean like breakfast, lunch and dinner? Yes, I do.
d Three, maybe four times a year.
e No, I don't. My wife is a vegetarian. I eat meat once a week, maybe.
f Yes, I do. I eat an apple every day.

GRAMMAR: present simple + *how often* + time expressions

Use present simple to talk about habits and routines.
Use *how often* to ask about habits and routines.
   How often do you have coffee?
Use expressions of time to talk about habits.
every
once a
twice a   *day, week, month*
three times a
never
Note: The word *never* goes **before** the verb.
   I **never** have breakfast.

> SEE LANGUAGE REFERENCE PAGE 58

1 Complete the diagram with the expressions from the box.

twice a week   every month   every year
three times a month   ~~never~~   ~~every day~~
once a week

NEVER

EVERY DAY

2 Complete the questions with the verbs in the box.

have   see   talk   go   sleep   wake

Family Habits
How often do you …
(1) *see* your grandparents/children?
(2) ____ lunch with your family?
(3) ____ on the phone with your mother?

Sleeping Habits
How often do you …
(4) ____ up after 11.00am?
(5) ____ to bed after midnight?
(6) ____ eight hours?

3 Work in pairs. Ask the questions in exercise 2. Answer with a time expression from the grammar box.

How often do you see your grandparents?
Twice a month.

SPEAKING

1 Work in groups of three or four. Create your own 'Healthy Living Survey'. Make questions. Use the surveys in the lesson to help you.

2 Do the survey in your group.

3 Present your results to the class.

Useful language

One person …
Two people …
Three people …
Nobody …

ENGLISH AROUND YOU: food labels

1 🔊 2.3 Read and listen to the English words from food labels. What are they in your language?

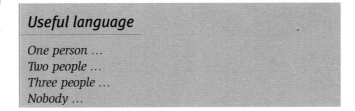

2 Do food labels in your country use English words? What words?

6D | Review

SPEAKING

1 Work in pairs. Say at what time you usually do these things.

I usually wake up at a quarter past seven.

2 Work with a new partner. Ask and answer questions about the activities.

What time do you usually wake up?

GRAMMAR

1 Look at the table and make sentences about Morning Meg or Nighttime Nick.

	go to bed late	wake up early	have breakfast	be late for work
Morning Meg	never	always	every day	hardly ever
Nighttime Nick	always	hardly ever	sometimes	three times a week

2 Match the question words and answers.

1 What?
2 Who?
3 Where?
4 When?
5 How much?

a The Rolling Stones!
b Free!
c The Ritz Hotel
d 9 o'clock
e A concert

3 🔘 2.4 Listen to the recording to check your answers. Make a similar dialogue.

VOCABULARY & LISTENING

1 Complete the menus with words.

Ricky's Diner

BREAKFAST MENU

Bacon

1 E_ _ _

2 T_ _ _ _ (brown or white)

3 Fruit (apple or o_ _ _ _ _)

4 Cr_ _ _ _ _ _ _

Coffee, tea or juice

Ricky's Diner

LUNCH MENU

5 Soup
(chicken or v_ _ _ _ _ _ _)

6 Sandwich
(ch_ _ _ _ _ or ham)

7 F_ _ _

Pasta of the day

2 🔘 2.5 Listen to the recording to check your answers.

3 🔘 2.6 Listen to a conversation in Ricky's Diner. Is it morning or afternoon?

4 🔘 2.6 Listen again and tick (✓) the food the man would like.

SPEAKING

Roleplay

1 Work in pairs, A and B.

A: You are the waiter at Ricky's Diner. Ask what B would like for lunch/breakfast.

B: You are a customer at Ricky's Diner. Say what you would like.

Useful language

What would you like for lunch/breakfast?
I'd like ...
Would you like ... or ...?
... please.
Here you are.

Self assessment (tick ✓)

In English ...

▢ I can ask the time.

▢ I can tell the time.

▢ I can say what I do on a typical morning.

▢ I know basic food vocabulary.

GRAMMAR

Present simple

The form of the verb is the same except for *he/she/it*. For *he/she/it,* add *-s.*

Affirmative		
I	live	
He/She/It	lives	in New York.
You/We/They	live	

Spelling: present simple verbs with *she/he/it*
For most verbs: add *–s.*
   work – works   eat – eats   like – likes
   play – plays
For verbs ending in consonant + *y: -y* ➔ *–ies.*
   study – studies
For verbs ending in *-ch, -sh, -o:* add *–es.*
   do – does   watch – watches

Have is an irregular verb.

Have		
I	have	
He/She/It	has	a computer.
You/We/They	have	

Make the negative with *don't* + infinitive or *doesn't* (for *she/he/it*) + infinitive.

Negative			
I	don't		
He/She/It	doesn't	live	alone.
You/We/They	don't		

For questions, put *do/does* before the subject and the infinitive after the subject.

Question		
Do	I	
Does	he/she/it	work?
Do	you/we/they	

Answer these questions with short answers.
   Do you speak English?   Yes, I do.
   Does he have a big family?   No, he doesn't.

Short answer			
	I	do. don't.	
Yes, No,	he/she/it	does. doesn't.	
	you/we/they	do. don't.	

Question words

What, where, when, who, why and *how* are question words.
Put them at the beginning of the question.
   How *are you?*
   Where *are you from?*
   What *is his name?*
   Who *does she work with?*
   Why *do you like your job?*

And, but

And and *but* are conjunctions. Use them to link words, phrases or clauses.
And gives more information.
   *I have a computer **and** I use it.*
But shows a contrast.
   *We have a fax machine, **but** we don't use it.*

Adverbs of frequency

always	often/usually	sometimes	hardly ever	never

Use adverbs of frequency to say how often we do something.
   *They **always** go to bed late at night.*
Adverbs of frequency go before the main verb.
   *They **sometimes** drink a cup of coffee.*
Adverbs of frequency go after the verb *to be.*
   *Mornings are **often** very difficult.*
To ask about frequency, use *How often…?*
   How often *do you go to bed late?*
We can also use expressions of frequency to talk about how often we do things.
   every
   once a   day, week, month
   twice a
   three times a
These usually go at the end of a sentence.
   *I eat fish **once a week**.*

FUNCTIONAL LANGUAGE

Asking and saying email addresses

What's your email address?

@	at
.	dot
/	slash
com	com

Asking and saying the time

What time is it?

It's + time

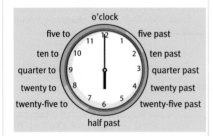

WORD LIST

Common verbs

dance *v****	/dɑːns/
drink *v****	/drɪŋk/
eat *v****	/iːt/
go *v****	/gəʊ/
have *v****	/hæv/
hear *v****	/hɪə/
like *v* ***	/laɪk/
live *v* ***	/lɪv/
play *v****	/pleɪ/
read *v****	/riːd/
sleep *v****	/sliːp/
wake up *v**	/ˌweɪk ˈʌp/
work *v* ***	/wɜːk/

Technology

computer *n****	/kəmˈpjuːtə/
digital camera *n*	/ˌdɪdʒətl ˈkæmrə/
email address *n*	/ˈiːmeɪl əˌdres/
fax machine *n*	/ˈfæks məˌʃiːn/
mobile phone *n*	/ˌməʊbaɪl ˈfəʊn/
printer *n**	/ˈprɪntə/
website *n*	/ˈwebsaɪt/

Adjectives

bad *adj****	/bæd/
boring *adj***	/ˈbɔːrɪŋ/
difficult *adj****	/ˈdɪfɪkəlt/
easy *adj****	/ˈiːzɪ/
good *adj****	/gʊd/
interesting *adj****	/ˈɪntrəstɪŋ/

Sports & games

basketball *n*	/ˈbɑːskətbɔːl/
chess *n*	/tʃes/
football *n***	/ˈfʊtbɔːl/
golf *n**	/gɒlf/
tennis *n*	/ˈtenɪs/

Food

breakfast *n***	/ˈbrekfəst/
chicken *n***	/ˈtʃɪkən/
dinner *n****	/ˈdɪnə/
eggs *n****	/egz/
fish *n****	/fɪʃ/
fruit *n****	/fruːt/
ice cream *n*	/ˌaɪs ˈkriːm/
lunch *n****	/lʌntʃ/
meat *n****	/miːt/
milk *n****	/mɪlk/
pasta *n*	/ˈpæstə/
salad *n**	/ˈsæləd/
soup *n**	/suːp/
toast *n*	/təʊst/
vegetables *n****	/ˈvedʒtəbəlz/

Other words & phrases

afternoon *n****	/ˌɑːftəˈnuːn/
bus *n****	/bʌs/
early *adj, adv****	/ˈɜːlɪ/
evening *n****	/ˈiːvnɪŋ/
expert *n***	/ˈekspɜːt/
factory *n****	/ˈfæktrɪ/
flat *n***	/flæt/
genetic *adj**	/dʒəˈnetɪk/
language *n****	/ˈlæŋgwɪdʒ/
late *adj, adv* ***	/leɪt/
night *n****	/naɪt/
nobody *prn****	/ˈnəʊbədɪ/
people *n****	/ˈpiːpl/
person *n****	/ˈpɜːsən/
scientist *n***	/ˈsaɪəntɪst/
train *n****	/treɪn/

7A | Weekend city break

VOCABULARY: places in a city (1)

1 Match the words 1–9 to the signs A–I.

1 a train station   2 an airport   3 a museum
4 a hotel   5 a park   6 a castle
7 a bridge   8 a river   9 a beach

A  B  C

D  E F

G  H I

2 🔘 2.7 Listen to the recording to check your answers. Repeat the words.

3 Make sentences about your city. Use the words in exercise 1.

The train station is on King Street.
The castle is next to the river.

PRONUNCIATION: word stress (2)

1 🔘 2.8 Listen to the words and the stress patterns. Say the words.

□	□◦	◦□
train	castle	correct
park	river	weekend
	airport	thirteen

2 Put the words from the box in the correct column.

station   hotel   city   police   bridge   beach

3 🔘 2.9 Listen and check your answers. Say the words.

Come for a WEEKEND BREAK

Barcelona

Come to the Spanish city for a PERFECT weekend city break.

_____

There's a train every 40 minutes from the airport to Barcelona Sants train station. Taxis are 15–20 euros from the airport to the city.

_____

There are many hotels in the city centre. Email our office for information.

Sagrada Familia church

_____

There are lots of things to do in Barcelona. Go for a walk on the famous Ramblas. See the Sagrad⟨a⟩ Familia church and other buildings by the archite⟨ct⟩ Gaudi. If you like art, go to the Picasso museum in the old part of town. Watch a Barcelona footba⟨ll⟩ match in the city stadium Camp Nou. Barcelona is ⟨a⟩ Mediterranean city, and there are beautiful beach⟨es⟩ in and next to the city.

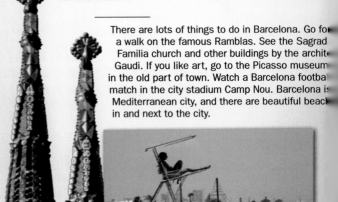

city beaches

READING

1 Look at the brochure. What do you know about these cities?

2 Read the brochure. Complete the blanks with the phrases below.

Where to stay   Getting there   Things to see and do

3 Read the brochure again. Mark the sentences B for Barcelona and P for Prague.

1 ____ There are beaches.
2 ____ There's a river.
3 ____ There's a train to the airport.
4 ____ There's a museum with Picasso art.
5 ____ There's a Mozart music show.
6 ____ There's an old bridge.
7 ____ There's a castle.

4 Do you know Barcelona or Prague? Would you like to visit these cities for a weekend break?

This week we look at two popular cities: one in Spain and one in the Czech Republic.

Prague

Wake up Saturday morning in the BEAUTIFUL capital of the Czech Republic.

Prague Castle

There's an international airport next to the city and taxis are 600 CZK. There are also buses at the airport.

Stay in Prague's beautiful hotels in the city centre. You can also stay in one of the old apartments near the river. Email our office for more details.

Look at the statues on Charles Bridge. Go for a walk in the old city and next to the beautiful river Vltava. See Prague Castle, one of the oldest castles in Europe. For music lovers, there is a puppet show of Mozart's opera, the Magic Flute.

Charles Bridge

GRAMMAR: *there is/there are* (1)

Use *there is/there are* to talk about existence of things.
There is + *a/an* + singular noun
   There is *an airport.*
There are + plural noun
   There are *buses from the airport to the city.*

> SEE LANGUAGE REFERENCE PAGE 76

1 Underline the correct word in these sentences.

In the classroom …
1 … there *is / are* twenty students.
2 … there *is / are* a teacher.
3 … there *is / are* three windows.
4 … there *is / are* one door.
5 … there *is / are* thirty desks.

2 🌐 2.10 Listen to the recording to check your answers. Repeat the words. Make the sentences true for your classroom.

3 Look at the information about St Petersburg, Russia. Make sentences with *There is/There are* and the words in **bold**.

There is an international airport.
There are buses and taxis.

ST PETERSBURG

Getting here
Pulkovo-2 international **airport**
Buses and taxis to city centre

Where to stay
Hotels and apartments in the city centre

Things to see and do
The Peter and Paul **Cathedral**
The (more than 300) **bridges** of St. Petersburg
The Mikailovsky **Castle**
Beautiful **parks** in Pushkin
The Hermitage **Museum**
The **Vodka and Caviar Bar** at Hotel Astoria

SPEAKING

1 Prepare a short presentation about a city you know. Use the phrases in the box to help you.

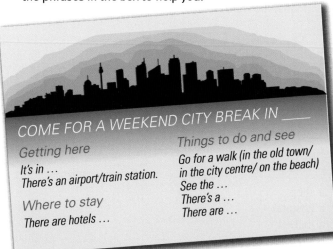

COME FOR A WEEKEND CITY BREAK IN ____

Getting here
It's in …
There's an airport/train station.

Where to stay
There are hotels …

Things to do and see
Go for a walk (in the old town/ in the city centre/ on the beach)
See the …
There's a …
There are …

2 Work in pairs. Present your weekend city break to your partner.

7B | A good neighbourhood

SPEAKING

1 Look at the picture of Lemmington. Work with a partner and make sentences.

There's a river.
There are two parks.

VOCABULARY: adjectives (2) places in a city (2)

1 🔘 2.11 Read and listen to someone talk about Lemmington. What are the red words in your language?

It's a small city.   It's beautiful.
Public transport is cheap.   The people are friendly.

2 Match the words in exercise 1 to the opposites below.

1 big
2 ugly
3 expensive
4 unfriendly

3 🔘 2.12 Listen to the recording to check your answers. Make the sentences in exercise 1 true for your city.

4 🔘 2.13 Find these places on the map. Listen and repeat the words

a shop
a hospital
a market
a supermarket
a bank

READING & LISTENING

1 🔘 2.14 Louis and Annie Walker are at the Lemmington Estate agency. They would like a new flat. Read and listen to the dialogue. What is the problem?

Mr Walker:	I'm Jeremy Walker. This is my wife, Annie. We're here about the flat.
Estate agent:	Ah yes. Nice to meet you. Well, Mr Walker, we have the perfect flat for you.
Mr Walker:	Oh. Is it near the city centre?
Estate agent:	Near the city centre? It's in the city centre!
Mrs Walker:	We have two small children. Are there any schools in the area?
Estate agent:	Oh yes, there are three schools.
Mrs Walker:	Is there a park?
Estate agent:	Yes, there is. In fact, there are two parks. This is a good neighbourhood for children.
Mr Walker:	And a hospital? Is there a hospital?
Estate agent:	Yes, there is. Look, there's a hospital here. Next to the river.
Mrs Walker:	Oh, that's good.
Estate agent:	There's also a market and there are very nice shops. And public transport is very good and cheap here too.
Mrs Walker:	Thomas, this is wonderful! One more question, how old is the flat?
Estate agent:	Errr … just a minute. It's … it's 83 years old.
Mrs Walker:	What? 83?
Estate agent:	Yes, well …
Mr Walker:	Look! Your website says *new* houses and flats.
Estate agent:	But it's very cheap.
Mr & Mrs Walker:	No, thank you. Good bye.

2 Read the dialogue again and decide if the sentences are true (T) or false (F).

1 The flat is vin the city centre.
2 There are three schools.
3 There are three parks.
4 There isn't a hospital.
5 Public transport is cheap
6 The flat is new.

GRAMMAR: *there is/there are* (2) (questions and negative)

Negative
Use *not* (*n't*).
There is a school.
*There **isn't** a school*

Question
Change the verb and the subject.
There is a hospital.
Is there *a hospital?*   *Yes, there is.*
               No, there isn't.

Use *any* with plural nouns in questions and negatives.
*There aren't **any** discos.*
*Are there **any** schools?*   *Yes, there are.*
               No, there aren't.

> SEE LANGUAGE REFERENCE PAGE 76

1 Rewrite the sentences. Use the symbols in brackets ().

1 There is a school. (?)
Is there a school?
2 There are shops. (-)
There aren't any shops.
3 There is a bank. (?)
4 There are parks. (?)
5 There are buses. (-)
6 There isn't a hospital. (?)
7 There aren't any shops. (+)
8 Are there any museums? (-)

2 Work in pairs. Ask and answer questions about your neighbourhood.

1 any shops?
Are there any shops? Yes, there are./No, there aren't.
2 a hospital?
3 a train station?
4 any beaches?
5 a hotel?
6 a bank?
7 any schools?
8 a market?

SPEAKING

1 Work in pairs, A and B.

A: Turn to page 115.
B: Turn to page 116.
Find three differences in your pictures.

"And this is the Sitting room and the Bedroom, and the Toilet, and..."

7c | In the city of York

The city of York is in the North of England. York is famous for its Roman and Viking history, and it is a popular destination for tourists.

LISTENING

1 Read the information about the city of York.

2 🔘 2.15 Listen to four conversations. Match the conversations 1–4 to the pictures A–D.

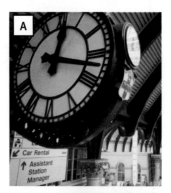

3 🔘 2.15 Listen again. Choose the correct answer.

Conversation 1
a) The train is at 4.45.
b) The train is at 3.45.

Conversation 2
a) There are tickets for the Mystery Play.
b) There aren't any tickets for the Mystery Play.

Conversation 3
a) The woman is from York.
b) The woman isn't from York.

Conversation 4
a) They are near the Castle.
b) They aren't near the Castle.

FUNCTIONAL LANGUAGE: survival English

1 🔘 2.16 Listen and complete the phrases in the box.

I'm (1) s____, I don't (2) sp____ English.
I don't (3) u____.
I only speak a (4) l____ English.
Can you repeat, (5) p____?
Do you (6) s____ German?

2 🔘 2.16 Listen again and repeat the phrases.

3 Look at the tapescript on page 123. Underline examples of the phrases.

4 Work in pairs. Choose one of the dialogues from Listening exercise 2 and practise.

VOCABULARY: travel words

1 Match the words to the pictures.

1 a map
2 a passport
3 luggage
4 a ticket (single/return)
5 a phrase book
6 a visa
7 money

2 🔘 2.17 Listen to the recording to check your answers. Say the words.

3 Imagine you are on a three-day-holiday in Britain. <u>Underline</u> five things you'd like to take with you.

a passport
a car
a visa
a bag
an English phrase book
a credit card
British money
a map
an identity card
a digital camera
a guide book for Great Britain

4 Work in pairs. Compare your lists.

I'd like a map, a visa, British money …

PRONUNCIATION: /m/, /f/, /v/ & /p/

1 🔘 2.18 Listen and repeat the sounds and words.

/m/ money
/f/ four
/v/ visa
/p/ passport

2 🔘 2.19 Listen and repeat the sentences.

1 My mother makes money at the market.
2 Fiona has forty-four favourite phrases in French.
3 Vincent needs a visa to visit the Vatican.
4 Peter uses public transport in Paris.

SPEAKING

1 Work in pairs, A and B.

A: You are a tourist in New York City, USA. You only speak a little English.
Turn to page 65.

B: You work at tourist information in Manhattan.
Turn to page 115.

ENGLISH AROUND YOU: signs

1 Look at these English signs. What do these words mean in your language?

2 🔘 2.20 Listen and repeat the words.

3 Are there any English signs in your city? What do they say?

7D | Review

SPEAKING & VOCABULARY

1 Work in pairs. Think of examples of …

> a small city
> a big, ugly city
> a good, cheap restaurant
> an expensive restaurant
> a beautiful old castle

2 Work with another pair. Read your examples. Can the other students guess the category?

GRAMMAR

1 The dialogue is missing five examples of *there*. Where do they go?

A: Can I help you?

B: I'd like some information about your hotel.

A: Yes, of course. What would you like to know?

B: Is a restaurant?

A: Yes, is. are two restaurants in the hotel.

B: Two restaurants. Thank you. Is a swimming pool?

A: No, I'm sorry, isn't.

B: Oh. No swimming pool. OK. Is the hotel in the city centre?

A: No, it isn't. We are 15 kilometres from the city centre. But are trains, and taxis. And we are very close to the airport.

B: Good. Thank you very much.

A: You're welcome.

2 🔘 **2.21** Listen to the recording to check your answers.

LISTENING

1 Match the words in the box to the pictures A–E.

> a phrase book   a passport   money
> a map   luggage

2 🔘 **2.22** Listen to four conversations. Match conversations 1–4 to pictures A–E. There is one extra photo.

SPEAKING

Travel game.

1 Work in groups of three or four. Play the Tourist Information game. You need counters and some dice.

1 Choose a city you know and write the name in the space.

2 You are all in the city. One person works at Tourist Information. The others are tourists.

3 The person at Tourist Information puts their counter in the middle.

4 The tourists put their counters on START. One tourist starts. The tourist rolls the dice and moves along the board.

5 If you land on a question square, ask the question to Tourist Information. Start your question *Excuse me …?* Tourist Information gives an answer.

6 If you land on a ⬜ square, it is the next player's turn.

7 If you land on a 🔀 square, change places with Tourist Information.

8 When you finish, it is the next player's turn.

9 Repeat stages 4–8 until all players finish.

Self assessment (tick ✓)
In English …
☐ I talk about where I live.
☐ I can say when I don't understand.
☐ I can ask for help in English.

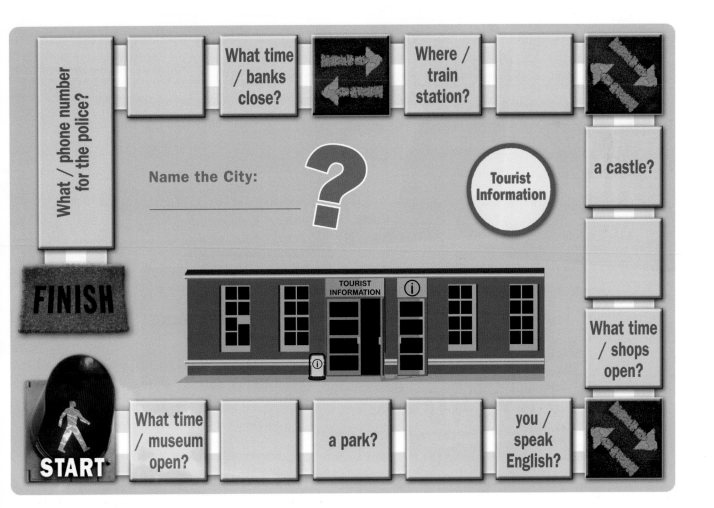

8A | Remakes

SPEAKING

1 Look at the film posters. Do you know them?

READING

1 Read the magazine article and match the pictures A–E in Speaking exercise 1 to the television shows or films. There is one extra picture.

REMAKES!

The number one rule in television and film is 'if it works, do it again'. Remakes are big business in Hollywood. We look at some popular remakes and their origins.

Charlie's Angels was a television programme of the 1970s. The 'Angels' were three women detectives. The Hollywood remake was in 2000. ____

The original *King Kong* was a 1933 film about a giant gorilla in New York City. *Gojira* was a Japanese film from 1954 about a giant monster from the sea. The Hollywood remakes were in 1998 (*Godzilla*) and 2005 (*King Kong*).

____

The *Mission Impossible* films with Tom Cruise (*Mission Impossible I* was in 1996, *II* in 2000 and *III* in 2006) were very popular. But the real *Mission Impossible* was a television programme from the 1960s and 70s.

____

2 Read the article again and complete the sentences with words from the text.

1 ____ are good for business in Hollywood.
2 ____ was a film from Japan.
3 ____ was a gorilla in New York.
4 ____ and ____ were Hollywood remakes in 2000.

3 Do you know the Hollywood remakes from the article? Do you like them? Tell a partner.

GRAMMAR: *was/were*

The past tense of *to be* is *was/were*.
Godzilla **was** a Japanese film.
Charlie's Angels *and* Mission Impossible **were** television programmes.

I/He/She/It	was
You/We/They	were

> SEE LANGUAGE REFERENCE PAGE 76

1 2.23 Listen and make the sentences in the past tense.

1 The film is at seven o'clock.
2 The tickets are expensive.
3 You are on the street.
4 It is cold.
5 I am late.
6 You are angry.

2 Complete the texts about television shows and films with the verb *to be* in the past.

1 The first James Bond film ____ *Dr No* (1962). The actor Sean Connery ____ James Bond.
2 *Bewitched* ____ a television programme from the 1960s. Nicole Kidman was in the 2005 Hollywood remake.
3 The original *Star Trek* ____ on television from 1966 to 1969.
4 The American television programmes *X-files* and *Friends* ____ very popular in the 1990s.
5 *The Lord of the Rings* ____ a book by JRR Tolkein before it ____ a series of Hollywood films.

VOCABULARY & PRONUNCIATION: years

1 2.24 Listen and repeat the years.

2008	two thousand and eight
2000	two thousand
1954	nineteen fifty-four
2010	two thousand and ten
1960s	the nineteen sixties

2 Say these years.

1	1889	2	1962
3	1984	4	1977
5	1926	6	2014
7	2009	8	1930

3 2.25 Listen and complete the sentences with a year from exercise 2. When were they born?

Marilyn Monroe
Charlie Chaplin
Jodie Foster   was born in …
Clint Eastwood
Orlando Bloom
Scarlett Johanssen

4 Work in pairs. Repeat the sentences in exercise 3.

SPEAKING

1 2.26 Read and listen to the text.

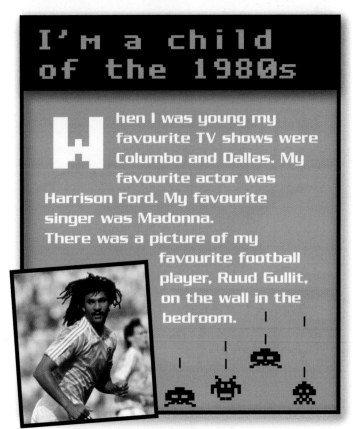

I'M A CHILD OF THE 1980s

When I was young my favourite TV shows were Columbo and Dallas. My favourite actor was Harrison Ford. My favourite singer was Madonna. There was a picture of my favourite football player, Ruud Gullit, on the wall in the bedroom.

2 Work in pairs. Make a similar text about your partner. Don't ask questions, guess.

3 Read your sentences to your partner. Were you correct?

4 Now work with another student. Talk about your partner.

Gabriela is a child of the 1990s. When she was young …

8B | Crime Scene!

READING

1 🔘 **2.27** Listen and match the words to the pictures A–C.

Fire!   Help!   Look out!

2 You are going to read a dialogue from a TV programme, *Crime Scene*. Check you understand these words.

dead   blood   fingerprints   lawyer   divorced

3 🔘 **2.28** Read and listen to the dialogue. Answer the questions.

1 What do John Kellerman and Dana Diaz do?
2 Does Mr Magnus know Peter Gordon?

Kellerman: Mr Magnus. My name's John Kellerman, and this is Dana Diaz. She works with the Crime Scene department.

Magnus: Well, nice to meet you, but I don't know what this is all about. Why am I here?

Diaz: Mr Magnus, do you know Peter Gordon?

Magnus: Yes, I do. We work at the same factory.

Kellerman: Mr Magnus. I have some bad news. Mr Gordon is … dead.

Magnus: That's impossible! He was at the factory yesterday!

Diaz: There was a fire at the factory last night Mr Magnus.

Kellerman: Where were you at 8 o'clock last night?

Magnus: Ummm, I was at home.

Kellerman: Really? Were you with somebody? Your wife?

Magnus: No, I wasn't with my wife. I'm divorced.

Diaz: That's right. Your wife, your ex-wife, was Peter Gordon's new girlfriend.

Magnus: Really?

Diaz: Mr Magnus, if you were at home, why were your fingerprints on the factory emergency exit?

Magnus: Wh … what?

Diaz: Yes, your fingerprints. And why was your blood on Mr Gordon's jacket?

Magnus: Listen, I wasn't at the factory last night and I wasn't with Peter.

Kellerman: Mr Magnus. You *were* at the factory. And you *were* with Mr Gordon.

Magnus: I … I …

Diaz: Do you have a good lawyer, Mr Magnus?

70

4 Read the dialogue again and decide if the sentences are true (T) or false (F).

1 Mr Magnus is dead.
2 Mr Magnus works with Peter Gordon.
3 There was a fire at the factory.
4 Mr Magnus wasn't at the factory yesterday.
5 Mr Magnus isn't married.
6 Mr Magnus' blood and fingerprints were at the crime scene.

GRAMMAR: *was/were* (questions, negative and time expressions)

Negative
Add *not* or *n't* to *was/were*.
  *I was**n't** at the factory.*
Question
The verb and the subject change places.
  ***Were you** at the factory?*
  *Where **were you** last night?*
Short answer
  Yes, I was.   No, I wasn't.
Time expressions
You can use these time expressions with the past.
  yesterday
  last night/week/month
Put them at the beginning or end of a sentence.

> SEE LANGUAGE REFERENCE PAGE 76

1 Rearrange the words to make sentences or questions.

1 you   friends   Were   Peter   with ?
2 factory   at   the   He   yesterday   was
3 fingerprints   door   Your   were   the   on
4 night   last   you   were   Where ?
5 factory   at   you   the   Were ?
6 her   last   night   with   wasn't   I

2 🔘 2.29 Listen to the recording to check your answers. Repeat the sentences.

3 Make questions with *Where* and the words and expressions in the box.

  last Friday night   last Sunday morning
  at 11.15 last night   at 5.30 yesterday

4 Work in pairs. Ask and answer the questions in exercise 2.

  Where were you last Friday night?
  I was at home.

SPEAKING

1 Play *Find someone who ...*

Move around the class. Ask *Were you...* questions. Answer *Yes, I was.* or *No, I wasn't.* Complete the spaces with names.

Were you in bed at 9 o'clock last night?
Yes I was.

Find someone who ...

... was in bed at 9 o'clock last night.
... wasn't in English class last week.
... wasn't in bed at 6.30 this morning.
... was at a party last weekend.
... wasn't at work yesterday.
... was at the cinema last cinema last Saturday or Sunday.

ENGLISH AROUND YOU: television

1 Read the names of famous English/American television programmes from recent years. Do you know these programmes? Do you like them?

| Crime Scene Investigation |
| Desperate Housewives |
| Lost |
| Big Brother |
| 24 |
| Survivor |
| Pop Idol |

2 What are these programmes in your language?

3 Which other American or English films/TV programmes do you know? What are their names in English?

That's my opinion

VOCABULARY: adjectives of opinion

1 Read the three texts and <u>underline</u> the adjectives.

A

Golden Dragon
Restaurant
Located on Centre Street, this Chinese restaurant has good food and the prices aren't bad. We recommend the Sunday lunch 'dim sum'.

B

ROBOT ATTACK !

★★★★ A great science fiction film!
Roger Dryden, Times

★★★★ Very very good. The action doesn't stop!
Duncan Foord, Independent Daily Newspaper

★★★ I like this film. I like it a lot.
Mercedes Grau, Latin film press

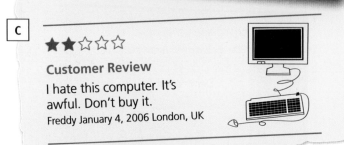

C

★★☆☆☆

Customer Review
I hate this computer. It's awful. Don't buy it.
Freddy January 4, 2006 London, UK

2 Complete the chart below with the adjectives from exercise 1.

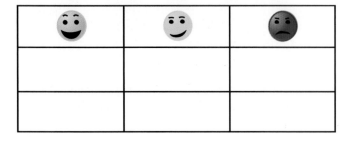

PRONUNCIATION: intonation (3)

1 🔘 2.30 Listen to the sentences. Are they positive or negative opinions? <u>Underline</u> the correct symbol.

1   3

2   4

2 🔘 2.30 Listen again and repeat the sentences. Copy the intonation.

LISTENING

1 🔘 2.31 Listen to people talk about their opinions. Match conversations 1–3 to texts A–C.

2 2.31 Listen again and <u>underline</u> the correct words.

1 The man *likes / doesn't like the computers / the food.*
2 The woman *likes / doesn't like the film / computers.*
3 The woman *likes / doesn't like the film / the food.*

FUNCTIONAL LANGUAGE: giving an opinion

1 🔘 2.32 Listen and repeat.

A: What do you think of the food?
B: I like it.
C: I think it's great.

2 Put the phrases in order on the diagram.

I like it.   I don't like it.   It's OK.

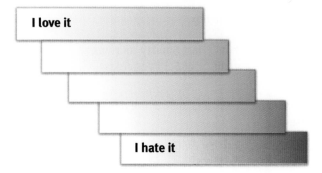

I love it

I hate it

3 Make sentences about the words in the box. Use the phrases from exercise 2.

science fiction films	football	computers
rock music cats	smoking	Chinese food

I like football.
I don't like rock music.
Science fiction films are OK.
I don't like smoking.

GRAMMAR: subject & object pronouns

Pronouns have two forms.
Subject pronouns
  He is an actor.
Object pronouns
  I like **him**.

> SEE LANGUAGE REFERENCE PAGE 76

1 Look at the tapescript on page 123. <u>Underline</u> all the object pronouns.

2 Replace the <u>underlined</u> words below with object pronouns.

1 Do you like Italian food?
  Yes, I love <u>Italian food</u>.
2 Do you like dogs?
  Yes, I like <u>dogs</u>.
3 Do you like golf?
  No, I hate <u>golf</u>.
4 Do you like mornings.
  Yes, I like <u>mornings</u>.
5 Do you like Brad Pitt?
  No, I don't like <u>Brad Pitt</u>.
6 Do you like Angelina Jolie?
  Yes, I love <u>Angelina Jolie</u>.

3 Work in pairs. Ask the questions in exercise 2. Give your own answers.

SPEAKING

1 Read the instructions to the game.

2 Work in small groups. Play the game.

Game: *That's my opinion*

1 Complete the circles with names of people or things that you know.
2 Work in small groups.
3 Ask and give opinions.

What do you think of Shakira?
I love her!
I think she's OK.

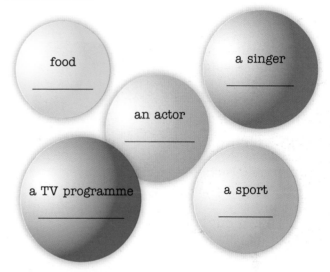

food _____

a singer _____

an actor _____

a TV programme _____

a sport _____

Useful language

What do you think of …?
Do you like …?
I like/love/hate it.
It's OK.
I think it's/they're great/good/bad.

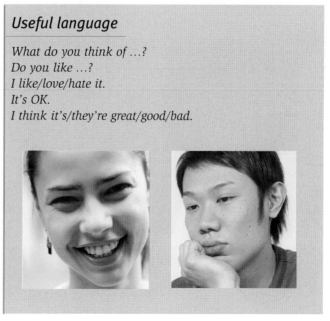

73

8D | Review

READING

1 Read the article about two actors.

1 Who was on television first, then in movies?
2 Who was in movies first, then on television?

From TELEVISION to the MOVIES and VICE VERSA
— a story of two actors

Keifer Sutherland is the son of actor Donald Sutherland. He was born in 1966, in London, UK. His first film was *Max Dugan Returns*. He was in other Hollywood films in the 1980s and 1990s, but he wasn't usually the main actor.  Keifer Sutherland is now most famous for the television series *24*.

 **George Clooney** is from Kentucky, USA. He was born in 1961. Clooney's father was a newsreader on television and George Clooney's first big acting job was in the television show *ER*. He was a doctor in that show. George Clooney is now a big Hollywood star, and was in many blockbuster films including *Batman and Robin*, *Ocean's Eleven* and *Syriana*.

2 Read the article again and answer the questions about each actor.

1 Where was he born?
2 When was he born?
3 What was his first acting job?

GRAMMAR

1 Choose the correct answer.

1 Please listen ...
   a) ... to me.
   b) ... to I.
2 Do you like the music group Coldplay?
   a) I don't know they.
   b) I don't know them.
3 Does you father speak English?
   a) He speaks a little.
   b) Him speaks a little.
4 She loves me, but I don't ...
   a) ... love she.
   b) ... love her.
5 They know us but we don't know ...
   a) ... them.
   b) ... they.

2 Put the words in the box in the correct order.

| yesterday | last night | this morning |
| last Saturday | last week | last March |

NOW

LAST YEAR

VOCABULARY

1 <u>Underline</u> the correct word for the dialogues.

1 A: Do you like it?
   B: No, I don't. It's *great / awful*.

2 A: What do you think?
   B: It's *beautiful / ugly*. I love it!

3 A: Teacher! Teacher! Look!
   B: Very *good / bad*, Barnaby. Everybody, look at Barnaby's work.

4 A: How's the weather today, Jim?
   B: The weather today isn't very *good / bad*.

2 🔊 2.33 Listen to the recording to check your answers. Read the dialogues.

FUNCTIONAL LANGUAGE

1 🔊 2.34 Read and listen to the text.

> In 2004, the British Council asked more than 7,000 students of English in 46 countries: What is the most beautiful word in English? Here are the top five words:

2 Do you have a favourite word in English? Complete the sentences with words you know in English.

1 I like the word …
2 I love the word…
3 I don't like the word …
4 I hate the word …

3 Work in pairs. Compare your sentences.

Self assessment (tick ✓)
In English …
▪ I can say when and where I was born.
▪ I can ask about likes and dislikes.
▪ I talk about things I like and don't like.

GRAMMAR

There is/there are

Affirmative		
There	is	a supermarket.
	are	two schools.

Negative		
There	isn't	a restaurant.
	aren't	any parks.

Question		Short answer
Is	there	a park?	Yes, there is. No, there isn't.
Are		any parks?	Yes, there are. No, there aren't.

Use *any* with plural nouns in questions and negatives.

> There aren't **any** discos.
> Are there **any** schools? Yes, there are.
> No, there aren't.

Past simple *was/were*

The past simple of *to be* is *was/were*.

> Godzilla **was** a Japanese film.
> Charlie's Angels *and* Mission Impossible **were** television *programmes*.

Affirmative & negative		
I He/She/It	was wasn't	on television.
You/We/They	were weren't	

Question		
Was	I he/she/it	in a film?
Were	you/we/they	

Time expressions

Use these time expressions with the past.

> *yesterday/last night/week/month*

Put them at the beginning or end of a sentence.

NOW

THIS MORNING

LAST NIGHT

YESTERDAY

LAST SATURDAY

LAST WEEK

LAST MARCH

LAST YEAR

Subject and object pronouns

Pronouns have two forms:

Subject pronouns come before the verb.

> *He is an actor.*

Object pronouns come after the verb.

> *I like him.*

Subject	Object
I	me
you	you
he	him
she	her
it	it
we	us
they	them

FUNCTIONAL LANGUAGE

Survival English
I'm sorry, I don't speak English.
I don't understand.
I only speak a little English.
Can you repeat, please?
Do you speak German?

I'm sorry, I don't speak English.

Giving an opinion
What do you think of the food?
I think it's great/awful.
I like it.
It's OK.
I don't like it.

WORD LIST

Places in a city
airport *n****	/'eəpɔːt/
bank *n****	/bæŋk/
beach *n***	/biːtʃ/
bridge *n***	/brɪdʒ/
castle *n***	/'kɑːsəl/
hospital *n****	/'hɒspɪtl/
market *n***	/'mɑːkət/
museum *n****	/mjuːˈziːəm/
park *n***	/pɑːk/
river *n****	/'rɪvə/
shop *n****	/ʃɒp/
supermarket *n**	/'suːpəˌmɑːkət/
(train) station *n****	/(treɪn) 'steɪʃən/

Things to take on holiday/Travel words
luggage *n*	/'lʌgɪdʒ/
map *n***	/mæp/
money *n****	/'mʌni/
passport *n**	/'pɑːspɔːt/
phrase book *n*	/'freɪz ˌbʊk/
ticket (single/return) *n****	/'tɪkɪt ('sɪŋgəl/rɪ'tɜːn)/
visa *n*	/'viːzə/

Adjectives
awful *adj***	/'ɔːfəl/
bad *adj****	/bæd/
beautiful *adj****	/'bjuːtəfl/
big *adj****	/bɪg/
cheap *adj****	/tʃiːp/
expensive *adj****	/ɪk'spensɪv/
favourite *adj***	/'feɪvrət/
friendly *adj***	/'frendli/
giant *adj*	/'dʒaɪənt/
good *adj****	/gʊd/
great *adj****	/greɪt/
nice *adj****	/naɪs/
original *adj****	/əˈrɪdʒɪnəl/
popular *adj****	/'pɒpjələ/
real *adj****	/'rɪəl/
small *adj****	/smɔːl/
ugly *adj**	/'ʌgli/
unfriendly *adj*	/ʌn'frendli/

Other words & phrases
actor *n****	/'æktə/
again *adv****	/ə'gen; ə'geɪn/
bar *n****	/bɑː/
blood *n****	/blʌd/
break *n***	/breɪk/
dead *adj****	/ded/
desk *n****	/desk/
detective *n**	/dɪ'tektɪv/
divorced *adj**	/dɪ'vɔːst/
ex-wife *n*	/ˌeks'waɪf/
fingerprint *n*	/'fɪŋgəˌprɪnt/
fire *n****	/faɪə/
impossible *adj****	/ɪm'pɒsəbl/
lawyer *n***	/'lɔːjə/
many *det****	/'meni/
opera *n*	/'ɒprə/
parking *n*	/'pɑːkɪŋ/
programme *n****	/'prəʊgræm/
public transport *n*	/ˌpʌblɪk 'trænspɔːt/
pull *v****	/pʊl/
puppet *n*	/'pʌpət/
push *v****	/pʊʃ/
remake *n*	/'riːmeɪk/
scene *n****	/siːn/
series *n****	/'sɪəriːz/
show *v****	/ʃəʊ/
statue *n*	/'stætjuː/
stay *v****	/steɪ/
stop *v****	/stɒp/
tour *n***	/tʊə/
wake up *v****	/ˌweɪk 'ʌp/
weekend *n****	/ˌwiːk'end/

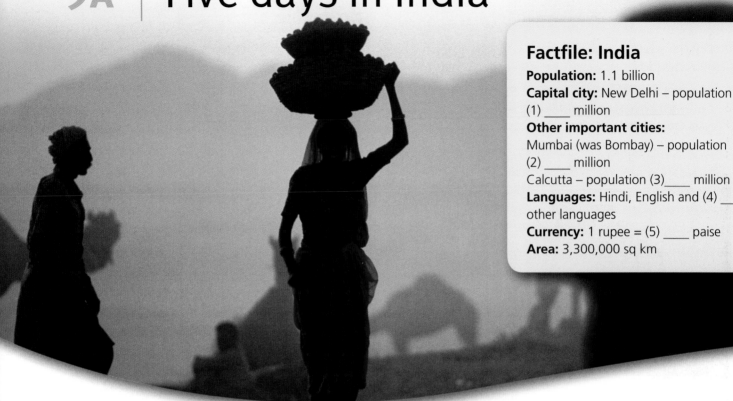

9A | Five days in India

Factfile: India
Population: 1.1 billion
Capital city: New Delhi – population
(1) ____ million
Other important cities:
Mumbai (was Bombay) – population
(2) ____ million
Calcutta – population (3)____ million
Languages: Hindi, English and (4) ___
other languages
Currency: 1 rupee = (5) ____ paise
Area: 3,300,000 sq km

VOCABULARY: big numbers

1   🔘 **2.35** Read and listen to the facts about India and complete the information with numbers.

2   Match the words and the numbers.

1	four hundred	a	400
2	a million	b	1,000
3	a hundred thousand	c	2,500
4	a thousand	d	10,000
5	a billion	e	100,000
6	two thousand five hundred	f	1,000,000
7	ten thousand	g	1,000,000,000

3   🔘 **2.36** Listen and repeat the numbers.

READING

1   Read Patti's email. Choose the correct answer:

1   This is an email for …
   a) … Patti's parents.
   b) … Patti's friends.
   c) … Patti's work.
2   The email is about …
   a) … Patti's job.
   b) … Patti's holiday.
   c) … Patti's family.

To:	d.vora@aol.com
Cc:	
Subject:	Last day in India!

Attachments: *none*   **B** *I* <u>U</u>

It's Friday! It's our last day in India and we're in New Delhi! We're fine, this is a quick email to tell you how we are.

Yesterday we were in the city of Agra. We saw the Taj Mahal of course. It was fantastic, but there were lots of tourists.
New Delhi is very big. The book says there are 11 million people here! Today we went shopping in the New Delhi markets. They are beautiful – but very crowded and noisy. We went to the National Museum, but it was closed.

Last night we went to a restaurant with some of Anne's friends. I ate a typical Indian dish, but I don't remember the name now. It had meat in it. I drank some Chai last night too! It's a kind of tea, and very popular here. Anyway, hope you and Dad are OK. There are many internet cafés here, so send me an email soon.

love
Patti

2 Read the email again and decide if the sentences are true (T) or false (F).

1 Yesterday they were in New Delhi.
2 There were lots of tourists at the Taj Mahal.
3 They went shopping in New Delhi.
4 The National Museum was closed.
5 Patti doesn't eat meat.

GRAMMAR: past simple irregular verbs (affirmative)

1 Find the past tense of the verbs in the grammar box and complete the table.

Present	Past
go	went
see	_____
eat	_____
drink	_____
have	_____

> SEE LANGUAGE REFERENCE PAGE 94

2 🔘 2.37 Listen to the recording to check your answers Repeat the words.

3 Rewrite the sentences in the past tense.

1 Every year, Michael and Violeta go to Poland for a holiday.
Last year, Michael and Violeta went to Poland for a holiday.
2 They go by plane from London.
3 They go to Warsaw.
4 They see their family and friends.
5 They drink Polish beer.
6 They eat Polish food.
7 They have a good time.

4 🔘 2.38 Listen to the recording to check your answers. Repeat the sentences.

SPEAKING

1 Read the text about a person's holiday. Where was he?

I was on holiday last August.
I ate pizza and spaghetti.
I drank red wine.
I saw the Coliseum and the Sistine Chapel.
I went to …

2 🔘 2.39 Listen to the recording to check your answer.

3 Prepare a similar text about a real or imaginary holiday.

I was on holiday last …
I ate …
I drank …
I saw … and …

4 Work in pairs, A and B.

A: Tell B your text.
B: Guess where A went on holiday.

5 Swap roles and repeat.

The Beatles' last day

READING

1 Do you know the English rock group the Beatles? Do you like them? Tell a partner.

2 The words in the box are all in the article. Check you understand the words. What do you think the article is about?

> group   studio   roof   building   crowd
> concert   legend

3 Read the article and check your answer to exercise 2.

• •

It was a cold day in January, 1969. On Saville Row in London, Paul McCartney, John Lennon, George Harrison and Ringo Starr were in the Apple Music studios. It wasn't a good time for the Beatles. They didn't want to work together anymore. They hated being in the same room together.

They decided to do something different.
Suddenly, the people in the street heard music. They didn't know what it was. They looked up and saw the Beatles on the roof of the building.
Cars stopped in the middle of the street. People got out and listened. Secretaries in the offices on Saville Row opened their windows. Soon there was a large crowd. It was a free Beatles concert!
The Beatles stayed on the roof and played their music to the street. Then someone called the police. The police came and stopped the concert.
The 1969 rooftop concert became a legend in English pop music. After the concert, the Beatles didn't play together again in public. It was the end of the sixties. It was the end of the Beatles.

4 Read the article again. Complete the sentences with words from the box. There are two extra words.

> police   holiday   friends   concert   cars
> roof   children

1 The Beatles' last ____ was in January.
2 The Beatles weren't good ____ at the time.
3 They played a concert on the ____.
4 People stopped their ____ and listened in the street.
5 The ____ stopped the concert.

GRAMMAR: past simple regular verbs (affirmative & negative)

> There are two kinds of past tense verbs in English.
> Regular e.g. *listen*   *listened*
>   The people **listened** to the music.
> Irregular e.g. *see*   *saw*
>   The people **saw** the Beatles.
> For regular past tense verbs, add -*ed* to the verb.
> Negative: *didn't* + verb
>   *They didn't play together again*
> Negatives are the same for regular and irregular past tense verbs.

⊙ SEE LANGUAGE REFERENCE PAGE 94

1 Find all the examples of past tense verbs in the text in Reading exercise 3. Which are regular and which are irregular?

2 Complete the sentences with the past simple of the verb in brackets.

1 The Beatles ____ (be) in the studio.
2 They ____ (not want) to work together.
3 They ____ (not like) each other.
4 They ____ (go) to the rooftop and ____ (start) a concert.
5 People ____ (look) up.
6 Secretaries ____ (open) their windows.
7 Someone ____ (call) the police.
8 The concert ____ (stop).
9 The Beatles ____ (not play) together in public again.

PRONUNCIATION: past tense regular verbs

1 🔘 2.40 Listen to the past tense regular verbs.

A		B	
work	worked	hate	hated
watch	watched	start	started
play	played	end	ended

2 🔘 2.40 Listen again and repeat. Which words have an extra syllable? A or B?

SPEAKING

1 Look at the history of the Beatles. Work in pairs. Make sentences. Tell the story of the Beatles.

A: *The Beatles were the most famous English rock group in history.*
B: *They were from Liverpool.*
A: *Their names were John, Paul, Ringo and George.*
B: *In 1957 John Lennon met Paul McCartney.*

ENGLISH AROUND YOU: songs

1 Many people learn English words from pop songs. Do you know these Beatles songs?

> Eight days a week   Yellow submarine
> HELP!   All you need is love
> Day in the life   Come together
> YESTERDAY   Let it be

2 What are these song titles in your language?

3 Do you know other English words or phrases from songs? What are they?

THE BEATLES

The most famous English rock group in history.

From:	Liverpool, England
Names:	John, Paul, Ringo, George

1957	John Lennon meets Paul McCartney.
1961	The Beatles play their first concert.
1962	The Beatles release their first song *Love me Do*.
1964	The Beatles visit America. They are no 1 in the charts.
1968	The Beatles go to India.
1969	The Beatles play their last concert.
1970	The Beatles make their last album *Let it Be*.
1980	John Lennon dies in New York.
2001	George Harrison dies.

9c | A national holiday

VOCABULARY: months

1 🔊 2.41 Listen and repeat the months of the year.

January	February
March	April
May	June
July	August
September	October
November	December

2 Work in pairs, A and B.

A: Say a month.
B: Say the month before and after.
A: *March*
B: *February, April*

3 What are your favourite months of the year? Tell a partner.

LISTENING

1 Look at the pictures of national holidays. What countries are these? Do you know these holidays?

2 🔊 2.42 Listen to two people talk about national holidays. Match the speakers to the photos.

Speaker 1 _____
Speaker 2 _____

3 🔊 2.42 Listen again. Who says it? Tick (✓) Sandra or Charlie.

		Sandra	Charlie
1	We have lots of holidays.		
2	I don't go to work.		
3	We got our independence from England.		
4	I usually have a big meal with my family in the evening.		
5	I always have a big barbeque with friends and family.		
6	It's a great day.		
7	There is always music and dancing.		

FUNCTIONAL LANGUAGE: the date

1 🔊 2.43 Listen and repeat.

A: What's the date today?
B: It's the fourth of July / It's July fourth.

2 🔊 2.44 With the date we use ordinal numbers. Listen and repeat the ordinal numbers.

first	eighth	twenty-first
second	ninth	twenty-second
third	tenth	twenty-third
fourth	eleventh	
fifth	twelfth	
sixth		
seventh		

3 💿 2.45 Listen and answer the questions.

1 _____
2 _____
3 _____
4 _____
5 _____
6 _____

PRONUNCIATION: /θ/ & /ð/

1 💿 2.46 Listen and circle the word you hear.

four	fourth
six	sixth
sink	think
day	they
dare	their

2 💿 2.47 Listen and repeat the sentences.

1 Today is Thursday the fourth.
2 The year is two thousand and thirteen.
3 Their mother is there.
4 I think it's her birthday.

GRAMMAR: prepositions of time (*in, on, at*)

> Use *in* with months, years.
> *in* 1776, *in* July
> Use *on* with dates, days.
> *on* March 5th, *on* Monday
> Use *at* with times.
> *at* 6 o'clock

> ❯ SEE LANGUAGE REFERENCE PAGE 94

1 Complete the sentences about national holidays with *in* or *on*.

1 South Africa's Freedom Day is _____ April 27.
2 Morocco has its national holiday _____ March.
3 India became independent from England _____ 1947.
4 Colombia's national holiday is _____ July 20.
5 Finland became an independent country _____ December 6, 1917.
6 Brazil's national holiday is _____ September.

2 Underline the correct preposition to complete the sentences.

1 My birthday is *in / on / at* June.
2 My English class finishes *in / on / at* 8 o'clock.
3 I never work *in / on / at* Sunday.
4 I was born *in / on / at* 1965.
5 The next holiday is *in / on / at* May 1st.

3 Make the sentences in exercise 2 true for you.

SPEAKING

1 Make questions with the words.

1 your country / have a national holiday? When?
2 you / like this day?
3 What / you / usually do / on this day?
4 What / be / some other important dates in your country?
5 What / be / your favourite day of the year?

2 Work in pairs. Interview your partner with the questions in exercise 1.

> ### Useful language
>
> *Our national holiday is on ...*
> *We usually ... have a picnic/go to a party/go on a parade/visit friends or family.*
> *We work/don't work on this day.*

9D Review

VOCABULARY

1 Which is correct? Circle a or b.

1 a) two millions
   b) two million
2 a) a hundred and ten
   b) hundred ten
3 a) two thousand four hundred
   b) two thousand and four hundred
4 a) fifty thousands
   b) fifty thousand

2 Work in pairs, A and B.

A: Write five big numbers. Don't show B. Read your numbers to B.
B: Write the numbers A says. Compare your numbers with the original. Were you right?

3 Swap roles and repeat.

LISTENING

1 🔊 2.48 Listen and complete the facts with a number.

The Beatles – by numbers!
Number of songs: (1) _____
Number of singles: (2) _____
Number of CDs: (3) _____
Number of Beatles live concerts: (4) _____
Number of copies of 1 sold in first month:
more than (5) _____

2 Check your answers with the tapescript on page 124. Say the numbers.

GRAMMAR

1 Complete the text with the past tense form of the verbs in brackets.

My first rock concert
I (1) _____ (go) to my first rock concert last August. I (2) _____ (be) in Berlin with my girlfriend. She (3) _____ (want) to see a new German group. We (4) _____ (get) tickets in the city centre. The concert (5) _____ (start) at 10 o'clock. We (6) _____ (have) dinner first, and we (7) _____ (arrive) at the concert at nine thirty. It (8) _____ (be) in a small club. The group (9) _____ (play) for two hours. It (10) _____ (be) very noisy. My girlfriend (11) _____ (love) the concert, but I (12) _____ (not like) it. I don't remember the name of the group.

2 🔊 2.49 Listen to the sentences. Are they past or present?

1 past present
2 past present
3 past present
4 past present
5 past present

3 🔊 2.49 Listen again and write the sentences.

READING & VOCABULARY

1 Read about the origin of the English names for the months. Complete each line with a month.

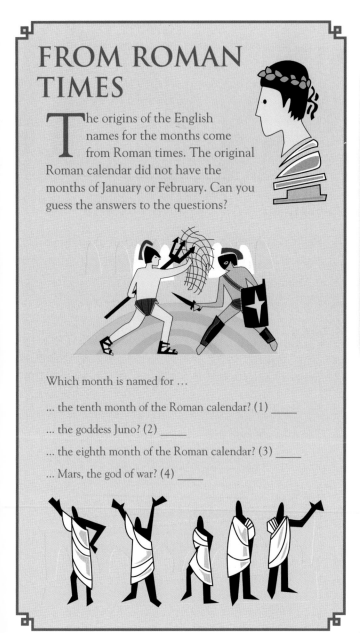

FROM ROMAN TIMES

The origins of the English names for the months come from Roman times. The original Roman calendar did not have the months of January or February. Can you guess the answers to the questions?

Which month is named for …

… the tenth month of the Roman calendar? (1) _____

… the goddess Juno? (2) _____

… the eighth month of the Roman calendar? (3) _____

… Mars, the god of war? (4) _____

FUNCTIONAL LANGUAGE

1 Work in pairs, A and B.

A: Say one of the dates in the box.
B: Say why the date is important.
A: *January 26th.*
B: *That's Burns Night.*

Important Dates
Great Britain

May Day	01/05
New Year's Day	01/01
Guy Fawkes Day	05/11
Rememberance Day	11/11
Boxing Day	26/12
Burns Night (Scotland)	26/01
Saint Patrick's Day (Ireland)	14/03

2 Swap roles and repeat.

SPEAKING

1 Think of two important dates in the year and write them on a piece of paper.

2 For each date, think of …

- … something you always do.
- … something you never do.
- … something you sometimes do.

3 Work in pairs. Tell your partner about your important dates.

Self assessment (tick ✓)
In English …
▢ I can understand and say large numbers.
▢ I can describe a holiday I had in simple language.
▢ I can say the date.

10A Did you have a good weekend?

VOCABULARY: weekend activities

1 Match the weekend activities 1–4 to the pictures A–C. One activity is not needed.

1 clean the house
2 make a meal
3 go away
4 do the shopping

2 Complete with words from the box.

do	make	go	clean

At the weekend I usually …

1 … ____ away.
          out.

2 … ____ a big breakfast.
          dinner for my family.

3 … ____ the house.
          the car.

4 … ____ the shopping.
          nothing.

3 🔘 2.50 Listen to the recording to check your answers. Repeat the phrases.

4 Complete the sentences so they are true for you. Use the phrases from exercise 1.

At the weekend   I usually …
                  I never …
                  I sometimes …

5 Work in pairs. Compare your answers to exercise 4.

LISTENING

1 🔘 2.51 Listen to a man and woman talk about their weekends. Tick (✓) the phrases you hear.

1 did nothing much
2 went to the disco
3 did the shopping
4 saw a film
5 saw the football match
6 went away
7 went to Rome

2 🔘 2.51 Listen again and choose the correct answer.

1 The man cleaned …
   a) … his car.
   b) … his house.
   c) … his room.
2 The man …
   a) … did the shopping and watched TV.
   b) … did the shopping but didn't watch TV.
   c) … watched TV but didn't do the shopping.
3 The woman went …
   a) … to France.
   b) … to Italy.
   c) … to England.
4 The woman went away …
   a) … with her family.
   b) … with a man.
   c) … with a woman.
5 The woman had …
   a) … a boring weekend.
   b) … an awful weekend.
   c) … a good weekend.

PRONUNCIATION: diphthongs

1 🔊 2.52 Listen to the words and sounds.

/aɪ/	/eɪ/	/aʊ/	/əʊ/
time	make	out	go

2 Put the words from the box in the correct column.

> break   house   wife   photo   train
> wine   play   no   nice   brown
> thousand   don't

3 🔊 2.53 Listen to the recording to check your answers. Say the words.

GRAMMAR: past simple questions (1)

> For questions in the past simple use the auxiliary *did*.
> *did* + subject + infinitive.
> **Did** *you go out?*
> **Did** *she have a good time?*
> Short answers
> *Yes, I did.   No, I didn't.*
> *Yes, she did. No, she didn't.*
> With *wh-* questions, put the question word
> in front of *did*.
> **Where** *did you go?*

> ➤ SEE LANGUAGE REFERENCE PAGE 94

1 🔊 2.54 Listen to the questions. Answer *Yes, I did* or *No, I didn't*.

2 Change the sentences to questions.

1 I went out after work.
   Did you go out after work?
2 I watched TV.
3 I used the internet.
4 I went out.
5 I did my English homework.

3 Make questions from the words.

1 what time / you / start work?
   What time did you start work?
2 what time / you / finish work?

3 how / you / get home?
4 where / you / go after work?
5 what / you / have / for dinner?

4 Work in pairs, A and B.

A: Ask B about last night. Use the questions in exercise 2. Answer B's questions.

B: Ask A about yesterday. Use the questions in exercise 3. Answer A's questions.

SPEAKING

1 Work in pairs, A and B. Have a conversation about the weekend. Use the diagram below and the useful language to help you.

A: Ask B, '*How was your weekend?*'.   B: Answer A.

A: Ask, '*What did you do?*'.   B: Tell A two things you did.

A: Respond.   B: Ask A, '*What did you do at the weekend?*'

A: Tell B one or two things you did.   B: Respond.

I went to the beach last weekend.

That sounds nice.

2 Now work with another student and repeat the conversation.

> ### Useful language
>
> **Responses**
> *Really?*
> *That's great.*
> *That sounds nice.*
> *That sounds awful.*
> *Oh no.*

10B | Pub Quiz

READING

1 Look at the pictures of a pub quiz in Britain. What do you think people do at pub quizzes?

a) Have a song and dance competition.
b) Ask and answer questions.
c) Talk about problems in the neighbourhood.

2 Read the text and check your answer to exercise 1.

A pub quiz is a popular game in Britain. People play the game in the pub. They work in teams. A person (the quizmaster) reads out a question and the teams write their answers on a piece of paper. At the end of the quiz, the team with the most correct answers wins a prize.

3 Are quiz games popular in your country?

FUNCTIONAL LANGUAGE: guessing

1 2.55 Listen to the two people at a pub quiz. Complete the sentences with a word from the box.

sure	think	maybe

Man: I (1) _____ it's Kiev.
Woman: (2) _____ it's Riga.
Man: No, I'm (3) _____ it's Kiev.

2 What do these phrases mean in your language?

3 2.55 Listen again and repeat.

LISTENING

1 Work in teams of three or four. You are going to play a pub quiz. Read the quiz sheet.

2 2.56 Listen to the questions and choose the correct answer.

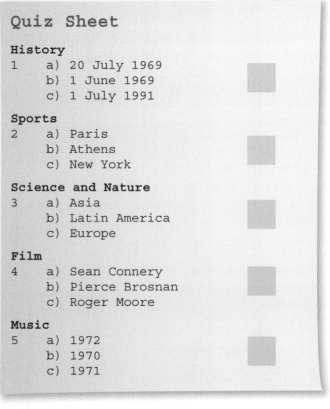

Quiz Sheet

History
1 a) 20 July 1969
   b) 1 June 1969
   c) 1 July 1991

Sports
2 a) Paris
   b) Athens
   c) New York

Science and Nature
3 a) Asia
   b) Latin America
   c) Europe

Film
4 a) Sean Connery
   b) Pierce Brosnan
   c) Roger Moore

Music
5 a) 1972
   b) 1970
   c) 1971

3 2.56 Listen again and check your answers with the others on your team. Then listen to the teacher give the correct answers.

GRAMMAR: past simple questions (2)

> Remember the word order for questions in the past.
> Questions with verb *to be*
> (Question word) + *was/were* + subject
> *Where was he born?*
> *Were you at the pub quiz?*
> Questions with other verbs
> (Question word) + *did* + subject + verb
> *Did you win a prize?*
> *What did you win?*
> For *yes/no* questions, remember the short answer form.
> *Yes, I was.*
> *Yes, I did.*
> *No, I wasn't.*
> *No, I didn't.*

> SEE LANGUAGE REFERENCE PAGE 94

1 Rearrange the words to make the questions from the pub quiz.

1 Neil Armstrong walk When on the did moon?
2 Where the first were modern Olympics games?
3 potatoes come from Where did?
4 James Bond Who first was the?
5 the Beatles end When did?

2 Make questions for another category using key words.

1 When / the USA / get / its independence from England?
2 What sport / Greg LeMond and Marco Pantani / do?
3 Where / the group Abba / come from?
4 Who / be / the author of Oliver Twist?
5 What year / the film Titanic / win 11 Oscars?
6 Where / Elvis Presley / come from?

3 Match the questions in exercise 2 to the answers.

a) Cycling
b) Charles Dickens
c) Mississippi, USA
d) 1821
e) Sweden
f) 1997

PRONUNCIATION: connected speech (2)

1 2.57 Listen to the sentences. How many words do you hear? (contractions = two words)

2 Look at the tapescript on page 124 and check your answers. Say the phrases quickly.

SPEAKING

1 Work in teams. Prepare five questions for a pub quiz. Use the words in the box to help you.

> When did …   Who was …
> Where was …   Where did … come from?
> Who was the author of …?

2 Work with another group. Take turns. Ask your questions. Answer the other group's questions.

10c Going shopping

SPEAKING & READING

1 Work in pairs. Do the shopping questionnaire.

Shopping questionnaire
1 Do you like shopping?
2 How often do you go shopping?
3 Did you go shopping last weekend?
4 What did you buy?
5 What are the best places to go shopping in your town?

2 Look at the pictures and read the text. What is it about?

a) The shop, Harrods
b) Places to go shopping in London
c) Things to see and do in London

The BEST shopping in the world

London is famous for Big Ben, Buckingham Palace, the river Thames and … the shops. Many people say that London is the best city in the world to go shopping. Here's a quick guide to our favourite shopping areas.

If you want big shops, go to Oxford Street. The department stores *Selfridges*, *Debenhams* and *Marks and Spencer* are there. For small boutiques, go to Kings Road or Portobello Road. Some of these shops are very expensive! The market at Covent Garden is a great place for old clothes.

Finally, a shopping visit to London is only complete when you visit the world-famous department store, *Harrods*, and get a special green shopping bag!

Glossary
a department store: a big shop that is divided into different sections, with each section selling different things
a boutique: a small fashionable shop

3 Read the text again and answer the questions.

1 Where is the market for old clothes?
2 Where are the department stores?
3 What place is famous for its bag?
4 Where are the small expensive shops?

4 Would you like to go shopping at these places? Tell a partner.

VOCABULARY: money and prices

1 Match the words to the prices.

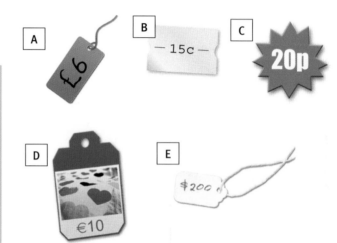

1 ten euros
2 fifteen cents
3 six pounds
4 twenty pence (twenty p)
5 two hundred dollars

2 🔘 2.58 Listen to the recording to check your answers.

3 🔘 2.59 Listen and repeat.

1 How much is it?
   It's $6.99
   It's six ninety-nine./six dollars and ninety-nine cents.
2 How much is it?
   It's €3.50
   It's three fifty./three euros and fifty cents.
3 How much is it?
   It's £25.59
   It's twenty-five fifty-nine./twenty-five pounds and fifty-nine p.

4 Work in pairs, A and B. Look at page 91. Practise asking for prices.

LISTENING

1 🔘 2.60 Listen and match the conversations 1–4 to the pictures A–D.

1 ____   2 ____

3 ____   4 ____

2 🔘 2.60 Listen again. Complete the phrases with words from the box

| where | help | bag | credit card | excuse |
| thanks | six hundred | | | |

1
A: Hello, can I ____ you?
B: I'm just looking, ____.

2
A: ____ me?
B: Yes?
A: ____ are the changing rooms?

3
A: How much is this?
B: It's ____ pounds.
C: I love it.
A: Can I pay by ____?

4
A: Would you like a ____ for that?
B: Yes please.

FUNCTIONAL LANGUAGE: in a shop

1 Who says it? Mark the sentences C for customer and SA for the shop assistant.

1 ____ Can I help you?
2 ____ I'm just looking, thanks.
3 ____ Where are the changing rooms?
4 ____ How much is this?
5 ____ It's 600 pounds.
6 ____ Can I pay by credit card?

2 Work in pairs. Look at tapescript on page 124 and check your answers. Practise the conversations.

SPEAKING

Roleplay

1 Work in pairs, A and B.

A: Turn to page 119.
B: Turn to page 116.
Roleplay a shopping conversation.

ENGLISH AROUND YOU: clothes labels

1 Read the examples of English on labels. What are these words in your language?

2 Do you know any English words from labels or English shop names? What are they?

10D | Review

Vocabulary & Speaking

1 Complete the words and expressions in the table.

What do the British do at weekends?

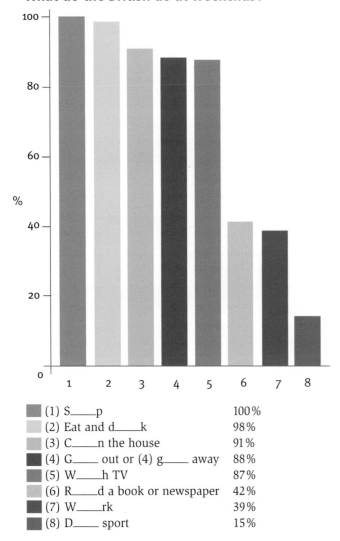

■	(1) S____p	100%
■	(2) Eat and d____k	98%
■	(3) C____n the house	91%
■	(4) G____ out or (4) g____ away	88%
■	(5) W____h TV	87%
■	(6) R____d a book or newspaper	42%
■	(7) W____rk	39%
■	(8) D____ sport	15%

2 Do you think these statistics are similar for your country? Make a list with a partner of popular weekend activities.

3 Work with another pair. Explain your lists.

Reading

1 Read the three texts about weekends. Match texts 1–3 to a person in the box.

the mother   the father   the son

What did you do this weekend?

1
This weekend wasn't very interesting. I played video games in my room. I talked on the phone to my friends. My Mum and Dad did nothing at the weekend, they only watched television on Sunday night.

2
On Saturday I did the shopping for the family. I made lunch for my son, he was in his room. On Saturday afternoon I cleaned the house. On Sunday I made lunch and dinner for the family. On Sunday night I watched my favourite television show with my husband. I was very tired.

3
I worked on the computer at home on Saturday morning. On Saturday afternoon I cleaned the car. I did nothing on Sunday, it's my rest day. I had lunch and dinner with my family and watched television with my wife in the evening.

2 Read the text again and complete the sentences with *The mother*, *The father* or *The son*.

1 ____ cleaned the house.
2 ____ cleaned the car.
3 ____ made lunch and dinner on Sunday.
4 ____ played video games.
5 ____ did nothing on Sunday.

3 Think of a typical weekend in your family. What do people do? Tell a partner.

GRAMMAR

1 Decide if the questions are correct or incorrect. If they are incorrect, correct them.

1 Did you away last August?
2 What did you have for breakfast?
3 How you come to class today?
4 What time you did wake up this morning?
5 Did you watch TV last night?

2 Work in pairs. Ask and answer the questions in exercise 1.

VOCABULARY

1 🔵 2.61 Listen and tick (✓) the price you hear.

1 a $16.15   b $16.50
2 a 200   b 2,000
3 a 80p   b 18p
4 a £1.99   b £199.00

2 Say the prices.

FUNCTIONAL LANGUAGE

1 Rearrange the words to make sentences.

1 book   this   How   much   is?
2 card   credit   I   Can   pay   by
3 25   It's   euros.
4 of   Yes   course.
5 I   Can   you   help?

2 The sentences in exercise 1 are part of a dialogue in a shop. Put the sentences in the correct order.

 5 ☐ ☐ ☐ ☐

3 🔵 2.62 Listen to the recording to check your answers.

SPEAKING

1 Look at the pictures of different objects. What are they? Work in pairs. Make guesses.

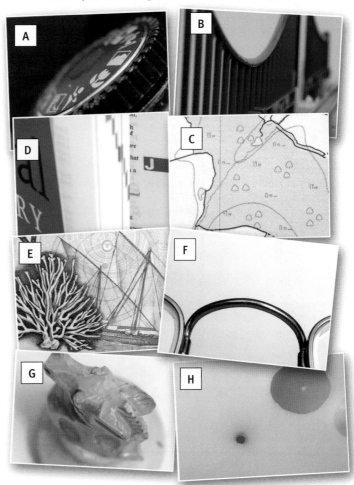

A
B
C
D
E
F
G
H
J

2 Look at page 117 to check your answers.

Useful language

I'm sure it's a/they're …
Maybe they are/it is …
I think it's a/they're …

Self assessment (tick ✓)

In English …
☐ I can say what I did last weekend.
☐ I can use language to make guesses.
☐ I can say prices.
☐ I can ask for prices and things in a shop.

GRAMMAR

Past simple

There are two kinds of past tense verbs in English.

Regular verbs: these verbs take *-ed* for the past simple.

> *walk – walked*
> *stop – stopped*
> *start – started*

Irregular verbs: these verbs change form in the past simple.

> *eat – ate*
> *go – went*
> *make – made*
> *see – saw*
> *have – had*

Many common verbs are irregular in the past tense. There is a list of irregular verbs on page 127.

Affirmative		
I You He/She/It We They	went	to India.

For negatives, use the auxiliary *did* and *not (didn't)* and the infinitive.

Negative			
I You He/She/It We They	didn't	go	to India.

For questions, use the auxiliary *did*. Put the auxiliary before the subject and the infinitive after the subject.

Question			
Did	I you he/she/it we they	go	to India?

Short answer		
Yes,	I you he, she, it	did.
No,	we they	didn't.

Prepositions of time
(*in*, *on*, *at*)

Use *in* with months, years.

> *in 2001*, *in July*

Use *on* with dates, days.

> *on April 4th*, *on Monday*

Use *at* with times.

> *at 6 o'clock*
> Note: *at the weekend*, *at night*

FUNCTIONAL LANGUAGE

Guessing

I think it's Kiev.
Maybe it's Riga.
No, I'm sure it's Kiev.

In a shop

Can I help you?
That's 600 pounds please.

I'm just looking, thanks.
Where are the changing rooms?
How much is this?
Can I pay by credit card?

Word list

Verbs

clean v***	/kli:n/
go away v***	/gəʊ əˈweɪ/
go out v***	/gəʊ ˈaʊt/
make v***	/meɪk/

Big numbers

hundred **	/ˈhʌndrəd/
thousand **	/ˈθaʊzənd/
million **	/ˈmɪljən/
billion	/ˈbɪljən/

Months

January n***	/ˈdʒænjʊrɪ/
February n***	/ˈfebjʊrɪ/
March n***	/mɑ:tʃ/
April n***	/ˈeɪprəl/
May n***	/meɪ/
June n***	/dʒu:n/
July n***	/dʒʊˈlaɪ/
August n***	/ˈɔ:gəst/
September n***	/sepˈtembə/
October n***	/ɒkˈtəʊbə/
November n***	/nəʊˈvembə/
December n***	/dɪˈsembə/

Money

cent n	/sent/
dollar n**	/ˈdɒlə/
euro n*	/ˈjʊərəʊ/
pence n	/pens/
pound n***	/paʊnd/

Other words

birthday n**	/ˈbɜ:θdeɪ/
boutique n	/bu:ˈti:k/
building n***	/ˈbɪldɪŋ/
clothes n***	/kləʊðz/
cold adj***	/kəʊld/
concert n**	/ˈkɒnsət/
crowd n***	/kraʊd/
crowded adj*	/ˈkraʊdəd/
department store n	/dɪˈpɑːtmənt ˌstɔː/
dish n**	/dɪʃ/
expensive adj***	/ɪkˈspensɪv/
free adj***	/fri:/
group n***	/gru:p/
independence n**	/ˌɪndɪˈpendəns/
last adj***	/lɑ:st/
roof n***	/ru:f/
shopping n**	/ˈʃɒpɪŋ/
shopping bag n	/ˈʃɒpɪŋ ˌbæg/
studio n**	/ˈstjuːdɪəʊ/
together adv***	/təˈgeðə/
world n***	/wɜ:ld/

11A | Artist, actor, athlete

Vocabulary: action verbs

1 🔘 2.63 Listen and match the verbs to the pictures. Repeat the verbs.

A

B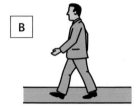

C

D

E

F

G

H

1 type   2 **sing**

3 dance   4 **run**

5 walk   6 *swim*

7 **drive**   8 play guitar

2 Cover the words. Look at the pictures and say the verbs.

People look at us and alway see what we can't do.

They don't think about what we can do.

A **The artist**
My name's Nathan. I work for a big company. I'm a graphic artist. I make websites. I can type fast – 114 words a minute!

B **The actor**
I'm Janice. I'm an actor. I can act, I c sing and I can dan I speak English, French and Spanis and I work on Broadway, New Y

Reading

1 Read the text about different people. What is it about?

2 Read the text again and complete the sentences with a name.

1 ____ uses a computer at work.
2 ____ knows many different languages.
3 ____ does sports.
4 ____ works with the internet.
5 ____ won a medal last year.
6 ____ works in the USA.

3 Each of the people in the text has a disability. Turn to page 118 to find out.

4 Do you know someone who has a disability?

c The athlete

My name's Isaac and I'm an athlete. I can swim and play tennis. Last year, I was in a national tennis competition. I won.

GRAMMAR: *can/can't*

> Use *can* + verb to talk about ability.
>   I **can** act.
> *Can* is the same form for all subjects.
>   *I/you/he/she/it/we/they* **can.**
> The negative of *can* is *can't*.
>
> **Questions**
> *Can* + subject + verb...?
>   **Can** *you dance?*
>
> **Short answer**
>   *Yes, I* **can.**   *No, I* **can't.**

⊙ SEE LANGUAGE REFERENCE PAGE 94

1 There are four mistakes with *can* in the text. Correct the mistakes.

> Our son Charles was born with cerebral palsy. Charles
>
> don't can walk, and he doesn't can run with the other
>
> children. But he can do lots of other things. He cans read,
>
> he can write his name and he can to use a computer.
>
> That's not bad for a four-year-old.

2 🔘 2.64 Listen to the recording to check your answers.

PRONUNCIATION: *can/can't*

1 🌐 2.65 Listen to the pronunciation of *can* in these sentences.

I <u>can</u> drive.	I <u>can't</u> drive.	<u>Can</u> you drive?
/kən/	/kaːnt/	/kæn/

2 🔘 2.66 Listen and write the sentences you hear. Practise saying the sentences.

SPEAKING

1 What can you do in English? Look at the phrases in the box. Put a tick (✓).

> ### *The English Challenge!*
>
> count to 20 ☐
>
> spell your name ☐
>
> say your email ☐
>
> say your phone number ☐
>
> introduce yourself ☐
>
> say what you did on Saturday ☐
>
> tell the time ☐
>
> say the date ☐
>
> describe the classroom ☐

2 🌐 2.67 Read and listen to the example.

A: Can you spell your name in English?
B: Yes, I can.
A: Show me.
B: M-I-C-H-A-E-L.

3 Work in pairs, A and B. Play the English Challenge game.

A: *Can you ... in English?*
B: *Yes, I can. / No, I can't.*
A: *Show me.*

11B Glastonbury

SPEAKING

1 Work in pairs. Look at the picture of the Glastonbury Festival and answer the questions.

1 What can you see?
2 Where are they?
3 Would you like to be there?

LISTENING

1 🔘 2.68 Listen to telephone conversations 1–4 at this event. Which conversation:

talks about food?   ____
talks about work?   ____
talks about clothes?   ____
is in the car?   ____

2 🔘 2.68 Listen again and choose the correct word to complete the sentences.

1 The woman is …
   a) … in front of the gates.
   b) … at the front gates.
2 Josh is getting something …
   a) … to eat.
   b) … to drink.
3 Rob is wearing …
   a) … a blue jacket.
   b) … a red jacket.
4 The woman is having …
   a) … a good time.
   b) … a bad time.

GRAMMAR: present continuous

Use the present continuous to talk about things happening now.
Subject + *to be* + verb + *-ing*
   I am driving.
Question
(question word) + *to be* + subject + verb + *-ing*
   What are you doing?
   Is it raining?
Negative
Subject + *to be* + *not* (*n't*) + verb + *-ing*
   I'm not working.

⊙ SEE LANGUAGE REFERENCE PAGE 112

1 🔘 2.69 Listen to the sounds and make a sentence with one of the verbs in the box. Use the present continuous.

have a shower   talk on the phone   drive
play guitar   type

1 He …
2 They …
3 She …
4 They …
5 She …

2 Complete the dialogue with the present continuous form of the verbs in brackets.

A: Hello?
B: Hello, darling, it's your mother. How are you?
A: Fine, thanks.
B: What ____ you ____ (do)? What's that noise?
A: I'm at a concert. The band ____ (play). People ____ (dance) and … it's a bit crazy.
B: Oh, that sounds nice. When does the concert finish?
A: What?
B: Darling, you ____ (not listen).
A: I ____ (listen), Mum, but I can't hear you! John and Liz ____ (talk) at the same time … Quiet, I ____ (use) the phone …
B: Hello? Hello? Oh dear, his phone ____ (not work) now.

3 🔘 2.70 Listen to the recording to check your answers.

PRONUNCIATION: /ŋ/

1 🔘 2.71 Listen and repeat the sound and words.

/ŋ/
thing
having
eating

2 Underline the words with the /ŋ/ sound in the sentences. Practise saying the sentences.

1 I'm going to the bank.
2 She's speaking French.
3 I can't think.
4 Is English a difficult language?

SPEAKING

1 🔘 2.72 Read and listen to the conversation. Match it to one of the pictures A–D.

A: Hi, how are you?
B: I'm fine.
A: Can you talk right now?
B: Yes, I can.
A: What are you doing?
B: I'm at home. I'm watching TV.

A

B

C

D

2 Work in pairs. Choose a different picture and make a similar conversation.

3 Roleplay your conversation.

ENGLISH AROUND YOU: international organizations

1 🔘 2.73 Glastonbury Festival is famous for its music, but also for social causes. Listen to the names of some well known non-governmental organizations.

2 Which organizations do you know? What are they in your language?

3 Do you know any other English names for international organizations? What are they?

11c | Britain's favourite paintings

SPEAKING & READING

1 Work in pairs. Look at the pictures and discuss the questions.

1 Do you know these paintings?
2 What do you think of them?

2 Read the article. What is the connection between the pictures?

3 Read the article again and answer the questions.

1 What was the competition about?
2 When was the competition?
3 Why did the National Gallery and the BBC organize the competition?
4 How many people voted?

4 Work in pairs. Ask and answer the questions.

1 Would you like to vote in an art competition?
2 Which picture would you like to win?
3 Is art popular in your country?
4 What artists do you like?

In 2005, the National Gallery of London and the BBC had a competition to find Britain's favourite painting. More than 118,000 people voted. The competition made people talk and think more about art. Here are some of the favourite paintings.

A Bar at the Folies-Bergère by Edouard Manet 1882

The Fighting Temeraire by John Turner 1839

Sunflowers by Vincent Van Gogh 1888

LISTENING

1 2.74 Listen to people talk about these paintings. Put the paintings in order you hear them.

2 2.74 Listen again and decide if the sentences are true (T) or false (F).

1 Van Gogh painted this while he was in France.
2 This painting is not very popular.
3 The woman is in Paris.
4 Maybe the woman is sad.
5 The Temeraire is a famous boat.
6 The Temeraire is the small boat.

FUNCTIONAL LANGUAGE:
talking about a picture

1 Read the sentences. Match each sentence to a painting on page 100.

1 In this picture I can see a woman at a bar.
2 The flowers are yellow.
3 There are two boats on the river.

2 2.75 Listen and repeat the sentences.

3 Make other sentences about the pictures on page 100.

Language note

Use the present continuous to talk about pictures.
*The small boat **is pulling** the big boat.*
*The men **are drinking**.*

SPEAKING

1 Look at another favourite painting. Make notes about what you see. Use the questions in the box to help you.

What can you see?   Where are they?
What are they doing?
What are they thinking about?

2 Work in pairs. Talk about the picture.

Mr and Mrs Clark and Percy by David Hockney 1971

11D | Review

LISTENING

1   2.76 Listen to a job interview. What is the problem?

2   2.76 Listen again and tick (✓) the correct sentences.

1 a The man can sing.
   b The man can't sing.
2 a The man can't dance.
   b The man can dance.
3 a The man wants a job at tourist information.
   b The man wants a job as a television actor.
4 a The man is in room 3.
   b The man is in room 4.

GRAMMAR & VOCABULARY

1   Make sentences about the people in listening exercise 1 in the present continuous affirmative or negative.

The man / stand.   *The man is standing.*
He / sit.   *He isn't sitting.*

1 The woman / listen to music.
2 They / talk.
3 The woman / look for a job.
4 The man / look for a job.
5 They / have lunch.
6 They / have a job interview.

2   Look at the pictures. Complete the sentences with *can/ can't* and a verb from the box. There is one extra verb.

run   eat   play   see   dance   drive

1 Sorry, I _____ .

2 She _____ fast.

3 He _____ tonight.

4 I _____ this guitar.

5 _____ you _____ me?

3   Test your memory. Cover the sentences. Look at the pictures and say the sentences.

4   Work in pairs. Complete the sentences so they are true for you.

We can …
I can … but my partner can't.
I can't … but my partner can.
We can't …

FUNCTIONAL LANGUAGE

1 Rearrange the words to make sentences.

1 Van Gogh think I a it's painting.
2 this picture in are four There men
3 I France think in it's
4 men are The sleeping.
5 I see can café this picture In a
6 Maybe New York in this is

2 Match each sentence to picture A or B. Say the sentences.

3 What do you think? Do you like these pictures? Ask and answer with a partner.

SPEAKING

1 Work in pairs, A and B.

A: Turn to page 114.
B: Turn to page 119.

Self assessment (tick ✓)
In English ...
☐ I can talk about what I am doing at the moment.
☐ I can describe a picture.
☐ I can talk about ability.

12A | Getting through

SPEAKING & READING

1 Work in pairs. Ask and answer the questions.

1 Do you like mobile phones?
2 Do you have a mobile phone?

2 Read the text about people and their mobile phones.

1 Who likes mobile phones?
2 Who doesn't like mobile phones?

Me and my mobile

This is my mobile phone. It has a camera, an MP3 player and a little television. It's very small. I love it. It's my fourth or fifth mobile phone. I change phones very often and I always have the new model.
Sara, Spain.

I have a mobile phone, but I don't use it often. I don't like them very much. I always forget to turn it off. And when I turn it off, I forget to turn it on again. The other problem is: when I want my mobile phone, I can't find it!
Clark, UK

My husband and I bought a mobile phone for our daughter. We thought it was a good idea. We could call her if we didn't know where she was. But now she uses it all the time to talk to friends and send messages. It's a lot of money, and who pays? Her parents! We don't think it's a good idea now.

Pavla, Czech Republic

3 Read the text again and decide if the sentences are true (T) or false (F).

1 Sara's phone is very old.
2 Sara changes phones often.
3 Clark forgets to turn on his mobile phone.
4 Clark doesn't use the mobile phone very much.
5 Pavla's daughter has a mobile phone.
6 Pavla doesn't pay for the mobile phone.

4 Are you similar to Sara, Clark or Pavla?

VOCABULARY: telephoning

1 Complete the sentences with the words in the box.

turn on	turn off	call	send

1 Please _____ your mobile phones in the cinema.
2 Can you _____ a text message with the information please?
3 After class I always _____ my phone and listen to the messages.
4 Sorry I didn't _____ you last night. I didn't have your phone number with me.

2 ⊙ 2.77 Listen to check your answers. Repeat the sentences.

LISTENING

1 Look at the picture of Clark. Answer the questions.

1 What is Clark doing?
2 Why is he angry?

2 🔘 2.78 Listen and put the phone calls in the correct order.

☐ Clark calls Sara's work.
☐ Clark calls the wrong number.
☐ Clark calls Sara's home.

3 🔘 2.78 Listen again and underline the correct words.

1 Clark *can / can't* use the mobile phone inside the building.
2 Clark phones the *right / wrong* phone number.
3 Sara *is / isn't* at work today.
4 *Clark / Sara* is at the library but *Clark / Sara* is at home.

PRONUNCIATION & FUNCTIONAL LANGUAGE
Intonation (4) (telephone English)

1 🔘 2.79 Read and listen to the phrases in the box.

Hello, this is Sandra.
Hello, it's Sandra.

Is that Mike?
Can I speak to Mike?
Is Mike there?

I'm sorry, Mike isn't here.
Can I take a message?
Would you like to call back?

2 🔘 2.80 Listen to five of the phone phrases again. Repeat the phrases and copy the intonation.

3 Cross out the incorrect option for each conversation.

	Hello.
	a) Hello, this is Clark. b) Hello, I'm Clark. c) Hello, it's Clark.
	Hello Clark.
	a) Is that Sara? b) Are you Sara? c) Sara?

	No, it's Paula.
	a) I can speak to Sara? b) Can I speak to Sara? c) Is Sara there?
	Just a minute. I'm sorry, Sara is a) here. b) not here. c) busy. Can I take a message?
	a) Please tell her I called. b) Please say her I called. c) Please tell her Clark called.

4 Work in pairs. Make conversations with the phrases. Pay attention to intonation.

SPEAKING

1 🔘 2.81 Read and listen to the dialogue. Match it to one of the pictures A–C.

Man: Hello.
Woman: Hello, is that George?
Man: No, it's Randall.
Woman: Is George there please?
Man: Yes, he is. Just a minute.
Woman: Thank you.
George: Hello?
Woman: George! When ARE you coming home? Dinner was ready at 8 o'clock!
George: Oh. Sorry. I'm in a meeting but I'm coming home now.
Woman: Hmph!

2 Choose another picture and prepare a similar dialogue.

12B | Departure lounge

SPEAKING

1 Look at the picture of the Airport terminal. Work in pairs, A and B.

A: Describe something you see.
B: Point to the part of the picture A describes.
A: *He's talking on the phone.*
B: *Here.*
A: *Right.*

2 Swap roles and repeat.

LISTENING

1 🔊 2.82 Listen to five conversations in the departure lounge. Match each conversation 1–5 to a letter A–E on the picture above.

1 ____
2 ____
3 ____
4 ____
5 ____

2 🔊 **2.82** Listen to the conversations again and answer the questions.

Conversation 1
1 What is Frank going to do?
2 What kind of film is it?

Conversation 2
3 Where is the man?
4 How is the man going to go to the hotel?

Conversation 3
5 How long is the man going to be away?
6 How often is he going to call the woman?

Conversation 4
7 Where is Nicky going?
8 Why is Esther going to Romania?

Conversation 5
9 Where is the woman going?
10 What is the problem?

3 Look at the tapescript on page 126 and check your answers. Choose one dialogue and practise.

GRAMMAR: *going to* (1) future plans

> Use *be going to* + verb to talk about future intentions.
> I'*m going to make* a film.
> I'*m not going to take* these bags.
> *Are you going to call* me?

> ❯ SEE LANGUAGE REFERENCE PAGE 112

1 Make a sentence in the future.

1 clean the house (-)   *I'm not going to clean the house.*
2 make a meal (+)   *I'm going to make a meal.*
3 go away (-)
4 do the shopping (-)
5 visit friends (+)
6 see a film (+)
7 visit family (-)
8 stay at home (-)

2 Make questions with the phrases in exercise 1. Interview a partner about the weekend.

1 *Are you going to clean the house?*   *Yes, I am.*

3 Complete the dialogues with *going to* + the verb in brackets.

A: Hi! What are you doing here?
B: I'm going to Siberia. My flight is in three hours.
A: Siberia?! What (1) ____ you ____ (do) in Siberia?
B: I (2) ____ (speak) at a conference. What about you?
A: I'm going to Italy. Again.
B: Family visit?
A: No, I (3) ____ (not see) my family this time. It's for work.

A: What's the purpose of your visit?
B: We (4) ____ (visit) friends.
A: Where (5) ____ you ____ (stay)?
B: At the Regent Hotel. Near the river.
A: OK, you can go.

SPEAKING

Roleplay

1 Work in pairs, A and B. You are friends. You meet at the airport terminal. Prepare a short conversation.

2 🔊 **2.83** Listen to the sound effects and have a conversation about your future holiday.

> **Useful language**
>
> *Hi! What are you doing here?*
> *What are you going to do?*
> *Where are you going to go?*

ENGLISH AROUND YOU: at the airport

1 Look at some English words from the airport. What are these words in your language?

2 🔊 **2.84** Listen and repeat the words.

3 Do you know any other international English words connected to transport?

12c | After the course

Home

Browse

Search

Invite

Mail

Blog

Favourites

Forum

Sign up

MY BLOG

June 16
Our course finished today. We all went to the park after the class and talked about our future plans. I'm a little sad because there aren't any more classes, but I'm happy because I have many new friends now. We're going to keep in touch, and of course we're going to see each other next year!
Here's a photo of all of us together.
I'm tired now, time for bed!
Tomorrow we're going to have our final exam!

View all blog entries

SPEAKING & READING

1   Work in pairs. Ask and answer the questions.

> When does your English course finish?

> Do you have a final exam?

> What are you going to do after the course?

2   Read the blog. What is it about?

1   the end of a course
2   the beginning of a course
3   a holiday

3   Read the blog again and answer the questions.

1   When did the course finish?
2   Why is the author happy?
3   When is the author going to see his friends again?
4   What is going to happen tomorrow?

VOCABULARY: feelings

1   Match the sentences to the pictures.

1 He's scared.
2 She's tired.
3 They're happy.
4 She's sad.
5 He's angry.

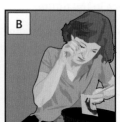

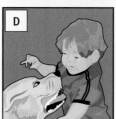

2   🔘 1.85 Listen and repeat.

3   Complete each sentence in two different ways.

I'm happy because …
I'm sad because …
I'm angry because …

108

GRAMMAR: *going to* (2); future time expressions

> We can use these time expressions with the future.
> *tomorrow*
> *tomorrow morning/evening*
> *next Tuesday/week/month*
> They go at the beginning or end of a sentence.
> *We're going to see each other **next year**.*
> ***Tomorrow** we're going to have our final exam!*

> SEE LANGUAGE REFERENCE PAGE 112

1 Put the time expressions on the diagram.

next Tuesday
next year
tonight
~~today~~
tomorrow evening
tomorrow morning
next month

2 Make questions with *going to*.

1 you / travel next year?
   Are you going to travel next year?
2 What / you / do next Friday?
3 Where / you / go after class?
4 you / study English next year?
5 you / come to school tomorrow?

3 🔘 2.86 Listen to some students talking at the end of their course. Check your answers to exercise 2.

PRONUNCIATION: *going to*

1 🔘 2.87 Listen how some words are stressed more in these sentences.

<u>What</u> are you <u>go</u>ing to <u>do</u>?
<u>Where</u> are you <u>go</u>ing to <u>go</u>?
<u>Are</u> you going to <u>call</u>?

2 🔘 2.88 Listen to the questions in Grammar exercise 2 again. <u>Underline</u> the stressed words.

3 Work in pairs. Ask and answer the questions. Pay attention to the stressed words.

FUNCTIONAL LANGUAGE: best wishes for the future

1 🔘 2.89 Listen and repeat the phrases.

Have a nice holiday!
Good luck.
See you next year!

2 Look at the table. Choose one or two phrases and memorize them.

Have a nice	weekend.
	summer.
	holiday.
Good luck with	the exam.
	your new job.
See you next	week.
	course.
	September.

SPEAKING

1 Work in pairs, A and B. Have a conversation. Follow the diagram.

A: Ask B's future plans.
B: Say two things you are going to do. Ask A's plans.
A: Answer B.
B: Give A best wishes.
A: Give B best wishes.
B: Say goodbye.
A: Say goodbye.

2 Close your books. Walk around the class and have a similar conversation with two other people.

12D | Review

SPEAKING

1 Work in pairs. Prepare a phone conversation. Use the diagram to help you.

A		B
Call B.	→	Answer the phone.
Say hello.		Say your name.
Introduce yourself.	→	Tell A that C isn't here.
Ask for C		Offer to take a message.
Say your message.	→	Say OK.
Say thank you.	→	Respond.
Say goodbye.	→	Say goodbye.

GRAMMAR

1 There is a word missing in each sentence. Insert the missing word.

1 I'm going to study English month.
2 I'm not going go away this weekend.
3 My family going to live in another country next year.
4 We going to have class next week.
5 The teacher not going to teach us next year.

2 Tick (✓) the sentences in exercise 1 that are true for you.

3 Work in pairs. Change the sentences in exercise 1 to questions. Ask and answer the questions.

VOCABULARY

1 Circle the wrong word in each group.

1	Beijing	Germany	Paris	Prague
2	four	seven	third	twelve
3	difficult	interesting	bad	bed
4	café	water	juice	tea
5	teacher	doctor	school	actor
6	red	medium	black	green
7	August	Monday	Wednesday	Friday
8	brother	mother	father	teacher
9	bridge	passport	supermarket	castle
10	cold	type	drive	sing

2 Work in pairs. Write your own Odd One Out exercise.

3 Work with another pair. Test each other.

FUNCTIONAL LANGUAGE

1 Match the expressions 1–8 to the pictures A–H on page 111.

1 What do you do?
2 What's this in English?
3 I'm sorry.
4 I'm just looking, thanks.
5 Excuse me
6 What time is it?
7 How old is he?
8 Fine thanks.

Are you going to study English next year?

Yes, I am.

A

B

C

D

E

F

G

H

2 🔵 2.90 Listen to the recording to check your answers.

3 Choose one of the pictures. Cover the words and role play the situation.

Self assessment (tick ✓)

In English ...

☐ I can answer the phone.
☐ I can leave a message on the phone.
☐ I can talk about future plans.

GRAMMAR

Can/can't

Can is a modal auxiliary verb. We use it to talk about ability.

Affirmative		
I You He/She/It We They	can	use a computer.

Negative		
I You He/She/It We They	can't	use a computer.

I can speak French.
Not ~~I can to speak English.~~
I can't dance.
Not ~~I don't can dance.~~

Question and short answer			
Can	I you he/she/it we they	dance?	
	Yes,	I you he/she/it	can.
	No,	we they	can't.

Can you hear me?
Not ~~Do you can hear me?~~
Can has different uses.
Use can to talk about ability.
  I can speak English.
Use can to ask for permission.
  Can I use your phone?

Present continuous

Use the present continuous to talk about events happening now or around now.
To form the present continuous, we use the auxiliary verb *be* in the present with the *-ing* form of the main verb.

Affirmative			
Full form		Contraction	
I am You are He/She/It is We are They are	talking.	I'm You're He's/She's/It's We're They're	talking.

Negative				
Full form			Contraction	
I am You are He/She/It is We are They are	not	listening.	I'm not You aren't He/She/It isn't We aren't They aren't	listening.

Question	
Am I Are you Is he/she/it Are we Are they	listening?

Going to future

Use *going to* + verb to talk about plans for the future.
  She's going to visit her parents in India.

Affirmative					
Full form			Contraction		
I am You are He/She/It is We are They are	going to	meet a friend.	I'm You're He's/She's/It's We're They're	going to	call.

Negative						
Full form				Contraction		
I am You are He/She/It is We are They are	not	going to	have a holiday.	I'm not You aren't He/She/It isn't We aren't They aren't	going to	have a holiday.

Question			Short answer
Am I Are you Is he/she/it Are we Are they	going to	have a holiday?	Yes, I am. No, I'm not. Yes, you/they/we are. No, you/they/we aren't. Yes, he/she/it is. No, he/she/it isn't.

With the verb *go* you can say *I'm going to go to the party* OR *I'm going to the party.*

Future time expressions

We can use these time expressions with the future:

tomorrow
tomorrow morning/evening
next Monday/week/month/year
Not ~~the next week~~

| NEXT YEAR |
| NEXT MONTH |
| NEXT TUESDAY |
| TOMORROW EVENING |
| TOMORROW |
| TONIGHT |
| TODAY |

FUNCTIONAL LANGUAGE

Talking about a picture

In this picture I can see a woman at a bar.
The flowers are yellow.
There are two boats on the river

Telephone English

Hello, this is Sandra.
Hello, it's Sandra.
Is that Mike?
Can I speak to Mike?
Is Mike there?

I'm sorry, Mike isn't here
Can I take a message?
Would you like to call back?

Wishes for the future

Have a nice holiday/weekend.
Good luck.
See you next year/month/September.

WORD LIST

Action verbs

dance *v****	/dɑːns/
drive *v****	/draɪv/
play *v****	/pleɪ/
run *v****	/rʌn/
sing *v****	/sɪŋ/
swim *v***	/swɪm/
type *v*	/taɪp/
walk *v****	/wɔːk/

Other words & phrases

blind *adj**	/blaɪnd/
blog *n*	/blɒg/
cerebral palsy *n*	/ˌserəbrəl ˈpɔːlzɪ/
change *n****	/tʃeɪndʒ/
competition *n****	/ˌkɒmpəˈtɪʃn/
deaf *adj***	/def/
disabled *adj**	/dɪsˈeɪbəld/
exam *n***	/egˈzæm/
find *v****	/faɪnd/
gallery *n*	/ˈgælerɪ/
guitar *n***	/gɪˈtɑː/
idea *n****	/aɪˈdiːə/
medal *n*	/ˈmedl/
message *n****	/ˈmesɪdʒ/
painting *n***	/ˈpeɪntɪŋ/
plans *n****	/plænz/
turn on *v****	/ˌtɜːn ˈɒn/
turn off *v****	/ˌtɜːn ˈɒf/
vote *v****	/vəʊt/
wheelchair *n*	/ˈwiːltʃeə/

Feelings

sad *adj***	/sæd/
happy *adj* ***	/ˈhæpɪ/
tired *adj* ***	/ˈtaɪjəd/
nervous *adj***	/ˈnɜːvəs/
angry *adj****	/ˈæŋgrɪ/

Communication activities

3A Speaking exercise 1 page 25

Student A

Read the information about the people.

Job File

Name	Country	Job	Phone number
Brad	the USA	firefighter	1 902 488 6521
Sue and Sean	England	police officers	44 208 445 8300

You start. Tell student B about the people in your chart.

Listen to student B talk about the people in his/her chart. Write the information in your chart.

5D Functional language exercise 1 page 49

Student B

Listen to Student A's addresses and write them down. If you don't understand, ask *How do you spell that?*

Read these email and website addresses to your partner.

martin991@mail.com

www.jobsincanada.com

hotel@online.com

www.visitlondon.com/information

11D Speaking exercise 1 page 103

Student A

Describe your picture to Student B. Find four differences in the pictures.

In my picture the man in the sunglasses is eating a sandwich.

4C Speaking exercise 1   page 37

Student A

Look at the picture. Don't show it to your partner.

Describe the picture to Student B.

Draw a ...
Next to the ... draw a ... .

7C Speaking exercise 1   page 65

Student B

You work at the tourist information office in Manhattan. Use the information for tourists below to help answer the tourists' questions.

Maps of Manhattan
colour map:	$5
black & white map:	$3.50

Tours
Central Park tour:	$17
Manhattan Movie tour:	$35
Statue of Liberty Boat tour:	$20

Broadway shows
Mamma Mia!
Phantom of the Opera
Chicago!
Special tickets:	$100

New York bus tours
Next bus tour: 5.15pm

7B Speaking exercise 1   page 63

Student A

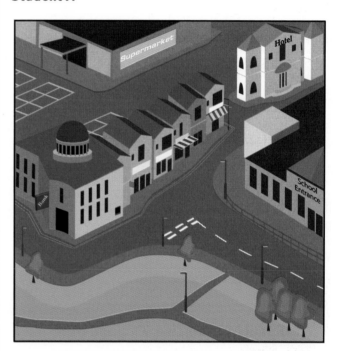

10C Vocabulary exercise 4   page 91

Student A

Ask about the object.

How much is (the computer)?

Student B

Say the price.

It's ($699).

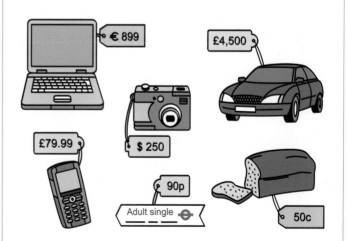

7C Speaking exercise 1 page 65

Student A

You are a tourist in New York city. You want information about these things:

- [ ] tour of Times Square?

- [ ] tickets to a Broadway show? / how much?

- [ ] a map of Manhattan? / how much?

- [ ] a bus tour? / what time?

If you don't understand, use the Functional English on page 64 to help you.

You start:

Excuse me, I'd like some information please.

10C Speaking exercise 1 page 91

Student B

You are a customer in the shop. Follow the instructions and have a conversation with A.
A starts

A:
B: Respond. Ask for the
   price for something.   *Yes. How much is this …?*
A:
B: Ask if you can pay
   by credit card.   *Can I pay by credit card?*
A:
B: Say thank you.
   Give the card.   *Thanks. Here you are.*
A:
B: Accept.   *Yes, please.*
A:
B: Say goodbye.   *Goodbye.*

Cover the words on the right. Repeat the conversation.

7B Speaking exercise 1 page 63

Student B

5D Functional language exercise 1 page 49

Student A

Read the email and website addresses to your partner.

www.maximum.com

sarah@hotmail.com

info@english.co.uk

www.sandwich.com/drinks

Listen to Student B's addresses and write them down. If you don't understand, ask *How do you spell that?*

4C Speaking exercise 1   page 37

Student B

Look at the picture. Don't show it to your partner.

Describe the picture to Student A.

Draw a …
Next to the … draw a … .

10D Speaking exercise 2   page 93

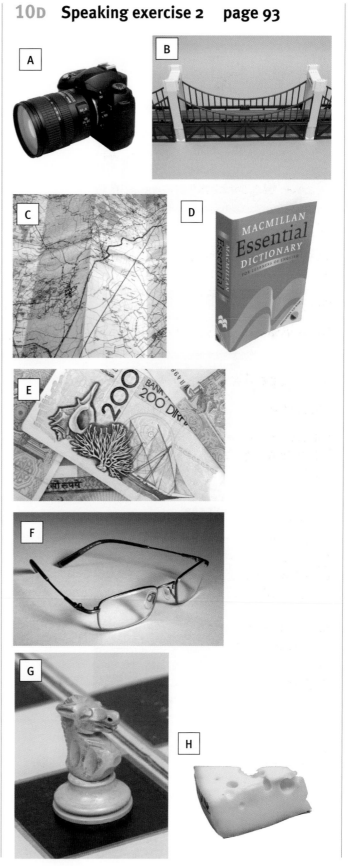

Nathan
He's deaf. He can't hear.

Janice
She's blind. She can't see.

Isaac
He uses a wheelchair. He can't walk.

Student B

Read the information about the people.

Job File

Name	Country	Job	Phone number
Michael	England	student	44 93 657 8845
Kanako	Japan	teacher	81 3 3499 8254

Student A starts. Listen to student A talk about the first person in his/her chart. Write the information in your chart.

Tell student A about the people on your chart.

10c   Speaking exercise 1   page 91

Student A

You work in the shop. Follow the instructions and have a conversation with B. You start.

A: Ask B if he/
   she wants help.   *Can I help you?*
B:
A: Tell B the price.   *It's…dollars, please.*
B:
A: Accept. Take B's card   *Yes, of course.*
B:
A: Offer B a bag.   *Would you like a bag?*
B:
A: Say thank you and
   goodbye.   *Thank you.*
B: *Goodbye.*

Cover the words on the right. Repeat the conversation.

11d   Speaking exercise 1   page 103

Student B

Describe your picture to Student A. Find four differences in the pictures.

In my picture the people are dancing.

2c   Functional language exercise 2 page 19

Work in pairs. Make dialogues with the words and pictures.

coffee: black or white?

juice: apple or orange?

mineral water: still or sparkling?

Tapescripts

1B   Listening exercise 1 💿 1.9

1   My name is Polly. I'm from England.
2   This is Pierre. He's from Paris, France.
3   Her name's Sofia. She's from Italy.
4   His name's Michael. He's from the USA.
5   Where are you from?
     We're from Germany.
6   This is Nikita and Igor. They're from Russia.

1C   Vocabulary exercise 2 💿 1.13

beep beep
beep beep beep beep
beep
beep beep beep beep beep
beep beep beep beep beep beep beep beep beep
beep beep beep

1C   Listening exercises 1 & 2 💿 1.14

1 M = man   W = woman

M: Oh, just a second … errr … sorry … a missed call.
W: You have one call from 623 485 531.

2 W = woman   W2 = woman 2

W: So, is there a message, any messages, for me?
W2:   Yes, James called.
W: Ahh. Did he leave a number?
W2:   Yes. 945 0782. It's on the table.

3 M = man

M: Yes … errr … can you call Mrs Kirsch and tell her she has a place in the 7pm … err … yes, 7pm English class? Her name is Kirsch and her number is 321 4510. Again, that's 321 4510.

4 V = voice

V: YES! Call our free number now for more information! The number is 1 888 962 962. That's 1 888 962 962. Call now.

1D   Functional language exercise 2 💿 1.20

1 M = man

M: Hi!

2 W = woman

W: Goodbye.

3 M1 = man 1   M2 = man 2

M1:   Nice to meet you.
M2:   Nice to meet you, too.

4 M1 = man 1   M2 = man 2

M1:   Hi! How are you?
M2:   I'm fine. And you?
M1:   Fine, thanks.

2A   Listening exercise 2 💿 1.21

R = receptionist   T = Tom

R: Hello. Welcome to the Berlin Palace Hotel.
T: Hello. I have a reservation.
R: What's your name please?
T: I'm Tom and this is Katy.

R: What's your last name?
T: Crewes.
R: Excuse me, Cruise?
T: Not the actor. My name's C-R-E-W-E-S.

2A   Vocabulary & pronunciation exercise 5 💿 1.25

1 M = man   R = receptionist

M: My name is Crewes.
R: How do you spell your last name?
M: C-R-E-W-E-S.
R: Oh. Thank you.

2 R = receptionist   V = Victoria

R: Welcome to the Berlin Palace Hotel.
V: I have a reservation. My name is Victoria Bickham.
R: Excuse me? Beckham?
V: No, Bickham.
R: How do you spell your name?
V: B-I-C-K-H-A-M.

2A   Vocabulary & listening exercise 2 💿 1.28

M = man   B = Birgit

M: Hello, Birgit. How are you?
B: Fine, thanks. And you?
M: I'm fine. Listen, I'm just checking the hotel rooms.
B: Just a minute. Mr Crewes is in room 14.
M: Yes.
B: Mrs Bickham is …
M: Mrs Beckham?
B: No, Bickham. She's in room 17.
M: And Mr and Mrs Woods?
B: In room 20.
M: Good.
B: And Ms Camilla Parker is in room 11.
M: Wonderful. Good work, Birgit.
B: Thank you.

2A   English around you exercise 2 💿 1.30

BBC   British Broadcasting Corporation
IBM   International Business Machines
CNN   Cable News Network
UK   United Kingdom
USA   United States of America
FBI   Federal Bureau of Investigation

2C   Listening exercise 1 💿 1.35

W = waitress   M1 = man 1   M2 = man 2   Wo1 = woman
Wo2 = woman 2   F = Frank

W: Yes.
M1:   I'd like two coffees please.
W: Two coffees, OK.
Wo1: A tea and a croissant, please.
W: OK.
M2:   Excuse me?

W:	Yes?
M2:	Two sandwiches.
W:	Would you like cheese or ham?
M2:	Cheese sandwiches, please.
Wo2:	Hello.
W:	Hi.
Wo2:	I'd like two teas, please, over here.
W:	OK, Frank? Two coffees, three teas, a croissant and two cheese sandwiches!
F:	OK!

2D Listening exercise 1 💿 1.40

1 M = man   W = woman

M:	So, where are you from?
W:	Cambridge.
M:	How do you spell that?
W:	C-A-M-B-R-I-D-G-E.

2 W = woman   M = man

W:	The hotel … ahh … it's wonderful.
M:	Where is it?
W:	In Torquay.
M:	Where?
W:	T-O-R-Q-U-A-Y. Torquay.

3 W = woman   M = man

W:	Mmmm … good cheese.
M:	Where is it from?
W:	Cheshire.
M:	C-H-E-S-H-I-R-E?
W:	Yes, that's right.

4 M = man   W = woman

M:	Write this down.
W:	OK.
M:	Greenwich. That's G-R-E-E-N-W-I-C-H. In England.
W:	OK, Greenwich.

3B Listening exercises 1 & 2 💿 1.48

M = Mike   D = Dominique

M:	Whew. Well. Hello.
D:	Hello.
M:	Do you speak English?
D:	Yes. A little.
M:	My name's Mike.
D:	I'm Dominique. Nice to meet you.
M:	Nice to meet you. Where are you from in France?
D:	Oh, I'm not French. I'm from Switzerland.
M:	Ah. Sorry.
D:	It's OK. Where are you from?
M:	The USA.
D:	Mmm.
M:	Excuse me?
D:	Yes?
M:	What time do we arrive in Madrid?
D:	Madrid?
M:	Yes.
D:	Oh no. This train is for Milan.
M:	What? But this is the Spanish Express to Madrid.
D:	No no no. This train isn't the Spanish Express to Madrid. This train is the Italian Express. The next stop is Milan.
M:	Oh no!

3C Listening exercises 1 & 2 💿 1.53

M1 = man 1   W1 = woman 1   W2 = woman 2
M2 = man 2

M1:	And that's the end of our tour of UNIS, the United Nations International School. Any questions? Yes?
W1:	When is the school open?
M1:	The school is open Monday to Saturday.
W2:	What is the school website?
M1:	It's www.unis.org.
M2:	Is the school cafeteria open every day?
M1:	No, it isn't. The cafeteria isn't open on Saturdays.
W1:	Where are the teachers from?
M1:	Many teachers at UNIS are from the United States, but we also have French, German, Swiss, Italian, Japanese and Australian teachers.
W2:	Are you the Director?
M1:	No, I'm not. I'm the Assistant Director.
W1:	Who is the Director?
M1:	The director is Mr Wye. He's in his office right now.

4A Listening exercises 1 & 2 💿 1.62

1 M1 = man 1   M2 = man 2

M1:	Hey, is that your car?
M2:	Yes, it is.
M1:	How old is it?
M2:	Well … it's forty-five years old.
M1:	Mmm … very nice.
M2:	Thank you.

2 W = woman   M = man

W:	Look! They're beautiful. Are they your babies?
M:	Yes. This is Fabio, this is Fiona and that's Lea.
W:	Beautiful! Hello! Hello! How old are they?
M:	They're fifteen days old.
W:	Awww. They're so young!

3 B = butler   M = man   W = woman

B:	Please come in.
M:	Oh, errr, thank you.
W:	Thank you.
B:	Follow me please. My master is in his room.
W:	How old is this house?
B:	This house is a hundred and one years old.

4 W = woman   M = man

W:	Hey, look, new computers!
M:	Well, not really.
W:	What do you mean?
M:	They're not new. They're from the London office.
W:	Oh.
M:	They're nine months old.
W:	Still … very nice.

4C Listening exercises 1 & 2 💿 1.71

L = Lee   M = Mark

1

L:	Hi Mark.
M:	Oh hello.
L:	Umm … where's my bag?
M:	What?
L:	My bag. My black bag.

M: I think it's on the table.
L: OK. No, it isn't.
M: Is it under the table then?
L: Oh yes, here it is.
M: Good.

2
L: Mark?
M: What is it?
L: Where are my glasses?
M: They're in your black bag.
L: No, they aren't.
M: In your jacket?
L: What jacket?
M: Your brown jacket. On the chair.
L: Oh yes, here they are.
M: Good.

3
L: Mark?
M: What now?
L: Where's my wallet?
It isn't in my brown jacket.
It isn't on the table.
It isn't in my bag.
M: I don't know where your wallet is! OK?
L: OK, OK.
Oh look! Here it is. It's on the sofa. Next to you.
M: Fine, here.
L: Thanks, Mark. Bye.
M: Bye.

4D Listening exercises 2 & 3 💿 1.72

US politics. It's a family affair. There are many famous families in American politics. Hillary Clinton, senator for New York, is ex-president Bill Clinton's wife. And of course, the Bush family. George W. Bush is George Bush Senior's son. And Jeb Bush and George W. Bush are brothers.

5B Listening exercises 1 & 2 💿 1.77

1 W = woman J = Jeffrey

W: I use email all the time. Not personal emails, though. Only emails for work. What about you, Jeffrey?
J: Oh, I don't know anything about computers or technology. I don't use emails, or the internet, or digital cameras.
W: No internet? Really? You're a bit anti-technology.
J: I have a mobile phone, but it's my brother's old mobile phone.

2 M = man W = woman

M: My wife knows all about computers. She works in an office.
W: Mmm.
M: She has, I think, two or three computers at work.
W: Two or three?
M: Yes, yes. We don't have a computer at home. She doesn't work at home … so no computer.

3 M = man W = woman

M: Is this the fax machine?
W: No it isn't. We have a fax machine here, but we don't use it. Everything is email now.
M: What is this machine?
W: It's a … it's a … you know … I don't know.
M: Mmm.

5D Vocabulary exercise 3 💿 1.84

M = man W = woman

1
M: OK, I'll give you my email address.
W: Just a minute. My pen … OK.
M: My email address is … it's hal006 at mail dot com.
W: Sorry, again?
M: h-a-l-0-0-6 at mail, m-a-i-l dot com.
W: Good. Thank you.

2
W: It's easier if you email me.
M: OK, what's your email address?
W: sofia, that's S O F I A at I-A dot net
M: I-A dot net. OK.

3
For more information, email us. Our email is mercedes at K-A-R dot com.

6B Listening exercises 1 & 2 💿 1.92

M = man W = woman

M: Hello, Chelsea Community Centre?
W: Hello, I'd like some information about the chess club, please.
M: Of course.
W: When does it meet?
M: Every Saturday. In the morning.
W: OK, Saturday morning. Err .. what time does it start?
M: At ten o'clock.
W: And … how much is it?
M: It's five pounds for the month.
W: Five pounds. OK, thank you.
M: Anything else?
W: Oh, yes. One more thing. Who do I talk to about the language classes?
M: Call the language school information number. It's 9023.
W: Thank you.
M: You're welcome. Goodbye.
W: Bye.

6C Reading & listening exercises 2 & 3 💿 2.2

I = interviewer M = man

I: Hi, excuse me. I'm doing a survey on eating habits. Can I ask you some questions?
M: Errr … yes OK.
I: Thanks. First question: Do you have three meals a day?
M: Do you mean like breakfast, lunch and dinner? Yes, I do.
I: OK. Question 2. Do you eat fruit and/or vegetables every day?
M: Mmm. Yes, I do. I eat an apple every day.
I: Do you eat meat and/or fish every day?
M: No, I don't. My wife is a vegetarian. I eat meat once a week, maybe.
I: How often do you have a meal at a restaurant?
M: Three, maybe four times a year.
I: How often do you eat with your family?
M: We have dinner together every night.
I: How often do you have lunch at work or school?
M: Well … I eat at home on Friday, but the other days I eat at work. So four times a week.

6D Vocabulary & listening exercise 2 💿 2.5

1

Right, this morning we have bacon, eggs, toast, fruit or a croissant.

2 W = woman   M = man

W: What's on the menu please?

M: Errr … soup – chicken or vegetable, sandwich – cheese or ham, fish or pasta of the day.

W: Oh.

6D Vocabulary & listening exercises 3 & 4 💿 2.6

B = Ben   Bk = Becky

B: Hello, Becky.

Bk: Hi there, Ben.

B: What time is it, Becky?

Bk: Errr … 1 o'clock.

B: Mmm. Time for lunch.

Bk: What would you like, Ben?

B: I'd like the soup.

Bk: Would you like chicken or vegetable?

B: Vegetable … no. Chicken please.

Bk: OK, chicken soup. And …?

B: And the fish please.

Bk: Chicken soup and fish. OK, Ben.

B: Thanks, Becky.

7C Listening exercises 2 & 3 💿 2.15

1 W = woman   M = man

W: Hello.

M: Hi, can I help you?

W: Yes, what time is the train to Newcastle?

M: The next one is at a quarter to four.

W: I'm sorry, I don't speak English very well. Can you repeat that please?

M: A quarter to four. Three forty-five.

W: Thank you.

2 M = man   W = woman

M: Excuse me, is this the tourist information office?

W: Yes, it is.

M: I'd like two tickets for the Mystery play tonight.

W: It's sold out.

M: I'm sorry, I don't understand.

W: There aren't any tickets for the play today. Come back on Friday.

M: On Friday? Oh, thank you.

W: You're welcome. Goodbye.

3 M = man   W = woman

M: Hello, is this the Jorvik Centre?

W: Excuse me?

M: Is this the Jorvik Centre?

W: I'm sorry. I only speak a little English. I'm not from here.

M: OK. Thank you.

4 M1 = man 1   M2 = man 2

M1:   Excuse me, I don't speak English very well. Do you speak Spanish?

M2:   No, I'm sorry I don't.

M1:   Is the castle near here?

M2:   Yes, it is. Do you have a map?

M1:   Yes, here.

M2:   Well, look. We're here … and the castle is over there.

M1:   OK, thank you!

M2:   You're welcome. Err … adios … heh, heh!

7D Listening exercise 2 💿 2.22

1

Aha, you see that there … that there's a map! Yes, matey, a map for the treasure they say … with an X that marks the spot. Aha!

2 W = woman   M = man

W: Excuse me?

M: Yes?

W: Your passport please.

M: Who are you? What is this?

W: Police. Your passport please, sir.

3 M = man   W = woman

M: So … ready, darling?

W: Yes, I think so. Urgh. Yep! Ready!

M: Is that your luggage?

W: Yes, darling. Why?

M: It's just that … it's a lot of luggage.

W: Yes, darling. It's our holiday!

4 M = man   W = woman

M: Excuse me?

W: Kann ich Ihnen helfen?

M: I'm sorry. I don't understand.

W: Kann ich Ihnen helfen?

M: I'd like an English-German phrasebook.

W: Sorry, can you repeat, please?

M: An English-German phrasebook. So I can understand you.

8C Listening exercises 1 & 2 💿 2.31

1 W = woman   M = man

W: What kind of food do you like?

M: Err, Chinese food. I love it. There's a Chinese restaurant near my house that has great dinners. It's good.

2 W1 = woman 1   W2 = woman 2

W1:   These are great.

W2:   What are?

W1:   The new computers. I love them. They're so easy. And beautiful.

W2:   I know.

3 M = man   W = woman

M: What do you think of the film *Robot Attack*?

W: Oh, please.

M: What?

W: It's bad. No, sorry, it's not just bad. It's awful!

M: Do you like the actor?

W: I don't know him. But science fiction films. Urgh. I don't like them.

9c Listening exercises 2 & 3 🔘 2.42

S = Sandra   C = Charlie

S: In Mexico we have lots of holidays. Our national holiday, our celebration of Independence, is in September. It celebrates the beginning of our fight for independence from Spain on September 16th, 1810. On this day I don't go to work. I usually have a big meal with my family in the evening. Then we go to the main square, the zocalo, for el grito. All the people shout 'Viva Mexico!'. There is always music and dancing. The party goes on very late into the night. Our Independence Day is never boring. I like it very much.

C: July 4 is Independence Day in the United States. We got our independence from England on this day in 1776. In my town there is an Independence Day parade, with music and flags. Same old story every year. I hardly ever go to the parade. But I always have a big barbecue with friends and family. A typical American barbecue, with hamburgers and coke. After the barbecue we often play a game of baseball. It's a great day. A great day just to be with friends and family really.

9c Functional language exercise 3 🔘 2.45

1 What's the third month?
2 What's the eighth month?
3 What's the first month?
4 What's the eleventh month?
5 What's the sixth month?
6 What's the second month?

9d Listening exercise 1 🔘 2.48

The Beatles … by numbers
The Beatles made an amazing number of songs. In total they had 217 songs, including 59 singles. There are at least 77 Beatles CDs.
The Beatles played in 1,400 live concerts.
And they hold the world record for most sales of an album. Their greatest hits album 1 sold more than 13 million copies in the first month.

9d Grammar exercise 2 🔘 2.49

1 He worked in a factory.
2 We hated the film.
3 I play tennis, watch TV …
4 The teacher wanted an answer.
5 She danced all night.

10a Listening exercises 1 & 2 🔘 2.51

W = woman   M = man

W: Hi, I want to tell you about my weekend.
M: OK.
W: But you first. How was your weekend?
M: It was fine.
W: What did you do?
M: Oh, I did nothing much.
W: Oh, well, because I …
M: I woke up late, cleaned the car …
W: Really? Interesting.
M: … did the shopping.
W: Mmm. Fantastic.
M: I watched TV.
W: TV. Great.

M: I saw the football match.
W: Do you want to know what I did this weekend?
M: What did you do?
W: I went away. To France. I went with Jacques.
M: Really. Did you have a good time?
W: Oh, it was great. We went to Paris. I loved it. He loved it. Would you like to see my photos?
M: No, thank you.

10a Grammar exercise 1 🔘 2.54

1 Did you go to the cinema last night?
2 Did you see a football match last night?
3 Did you read a book last night?
4 Did you go to a party last night?

10b Listening exercises 2 & 3 🔘 2.56

Q = quizmaster

Q: OK, OK. Quiet please. Ready for the quiz. These questions are multiple choice. I'll read the question and the possible answers. The first question is History. When did Neil Armstrong walk on the moon?
Was it:
a) on July 20 1969?
b) on June 1 1969?
c) on July 1 1991?
The next section is Sports. Where were the first modern Olympic Games?
a) Paris.
b) Athens.
c) New York.
Section three. Science and Nature. Where did potatoes originally come from?
a) Asia.
b) Latin America.
c) Europe.
Section four is Film. Our question here is: Who was the first James Bond?
a) Sean Connery.
b) Pierce Brosnan.
c) Roger Moore.
The last section is Music. Ready? When did the Beatles break up?
a) 1972.
b) 1970.
c) 1971.

10b Pronunciation exercise 1 🔘 2.57

1 Where did Mozart come from?
2 Who was the author of *Romeo and Juliet*?
3 When did Brazil get its independence?
4 What is the capital of Austria?
5 Who is the President of Russia?

10c Listening exercises 1 & 2 🔘 2.60

SA = sales assistant   C = customer   M = man   W = woman

1
SA: Hello, can I help you?
C: I'm just looking, thanks.
2
C: Excuse me?
SA: Yes?
C: Where are the changing rooms?
SA: They're over there. Behind you.
C: Thank you.

3

M:	How much is this?
SA:	It's 600 pounds.
W:	I love it.
M:	Can I pay by credit card?

4

SA:	Would you like a bag for that?
C:	Yes please.

10D Vocabulary exercise 1 🔘 2.61

SA = sales assistant   C = customer   Ch = child
M = man

1

SA:	That's 16.50 please.
C:	Sixteen dollars … and fifty cents. Here you are.

2

SA:	It's 2,000 euros.
C:	Two thousand? For shoes?
SA:	They are very good shoes, madam.

3

Ch:	How much is that sweet there?
M:	80p
Ch:	Oh. I only have 50p.
M:	Sorry.

4

On sale now, all CDs for 1.99, that's one pound ninety-nine!

11A Pronunciation exercise 2 🔘 2.66

1	Can you swim?
2	Yes, I can.
3	No, I can't.
4	I can't dance.
5	I can dance.

11B Listening exercises 1 & 2 🔘 2.68

1 M = man   W = woman

M:	Hello?
W:	Hi! Where are you?
M:	I'm in the car. I can't talk now though, I'm driving.
W:	I'm at the front gates. I have the tickets.
M:	OK. See you, bye!

2 W = woman   J = Josh

W:	Josh?
J:	Hello?
W:	Josh, what are you doing? We're waiting for you!
J:	I'm getting something to eat.
W:	What? I can't hear a thing.
J:	I'm eating! I'll be there in a minute.

3 R = Rob   Mi = Michelle

R:	Michelle?
Mi:	Rob? Where are you? I can't see you.
R:	I'm standing over here, near the stage. I can see you! Over here!
Mi:	Where?
R:	I'm wearing my red jacket! You're looking at me now!
Mi:	Oh yes, there you are! OK, I'm coming over now.

4 W = woman   M = man

W:	Hello?
M:	Hi. Are you at the office?
W:	No, I'm not working today. I'm at Glastonbury.
M:	Glastonbury? How is it? Is it raining?
W:	Yes, it is. As usual. But we're having a good time, anyway.
M:	Oh. Well, call me tonight, OK?
W:	Sure.

11B English around you exercise 1 🔘 2.73

Greenpeace
Fair Trade
Red Cross
Save the Children

11C Listening exercises 1 & 2 🔘 2.74

This painting is one of the most popular in Britain. Vincent Van Gogh painted these flowers when he was in France. The flowers are yellow, a symbol of happiness. Van Gogh painted more than eleven paintings with sunflowers.

In this painting I can see a woman. She is working in a bar in Paris. The amazing thing about this painting is the woman's eyes. I can't say how she is feeling. Maybe she's sad. Maybe she doesn't want to work there. There are lots of people behind her. They are drinking and having a good time.

The Temeraire was a famous warship in English history. In this painting we can see a small boat in front of *The Temeraire*. The small boat is pulling the big boat. The colour of the sun and the sea is very dramatic here. I really like this painting.

11D Listening exercises 1 & 2 🔘 2.76

M = man   W = woman

M:	Hello. Good morning.
W:	Good morning.
M:	I'm here for the job interview.
W:	Ah yes, yes. The job interview. Of course, come in.
M:	Thanks.
W:	Right. OK. I have some questions for you.
M:	Fine.
W:	Can you sing?
M:	Sorry?
W:	Sing … sing, you know, la la la.
M:	Errr … no, I can't. Not very well, no.
W:	Oh. Can you dance?
M:	What? Just a minute …
W:	Answer the question please, yes or no. Can you dance?
M:	No, I can't.
W:	You can't dance and you can't sing. What are you doing here?
M:	I'm here for the tourist information job.
W:	Tourist information job? Oh, no. That job interview is in room 4. This is room 3. This room is for television actor interviews.
M:	Ah, sorry.
W:	That's OK. Goodbye, then.
M:	Goodbye.

12A Listening exercises 2 & 3 🔵 2.78

C = Clark   SG = Security Guard   M = Man
P = Paula   S = Sara

1
C: Hmm … come on, Sara, where are you?
SG: Excuse me.
C: Yes?
SG: You can't use the mobile phone in the building.
C: Sorry.

2
M: Hello.
C: Yes, can I speak to Sara, please?
M: I'm sorry, you have the wrong number. There's no Sara here. This is MacDonald's.
C: Sorry…
P: Hello?
C: Hi. Is that Sara?
P: No, it's Paula.
C: Hi Paula, this is Clark. Can I speak to Sara, please?
P: Just a minute.
     I'm sorry, Sara isn't here. She isn't at work today. Can I take a message?
C: Yes. Please tell her Clark called.
P: OK.
C: Thanks, bye.
P: Bye.

3
S: Hello.
C: Is that Sara?
S: Hi, Clark.
C: Sara, where are you?
S: I'm at home. Why?
C: Well, I'm at the library. I'm waiting for you!
S: Oh no! I'm sorry. I forgot!
C: Doh!
S: I'll be there in half an hour.
C: Oh … alright then.

12B Listening exercises 1 & 2 🔵 2.82

1 J = Jenny   F = Frank

J: Frank, I'm Jenny from the Entertainment news.
F: Hi Jenny.
J: What are you doing here, Frank?
F: I'm going to make a film here.
J: What film?
F: It's a remake of a Hitchcock film.

2 W = woman   M = man

W: Where are you?
M: I'm at the airport.
W: Good.
M: What do I do now?
W: Go outside the terminal. A car is waiting for you. It's going to take you to your hotel.
M: Right.

3 W = woman   Ja = James

W: Oh, James.
Ja: Darling.
W: Am I going to see you again, James?
Ja: Yes, darling. It's only a week.
W: Are you going to call me?
Ja: Yes, darling. Every night.

4 N = Nicky   E = Esther

N: Esther!
E: Nicky! What are you doing here?
N: I'm going to Bangkok.
E: Bangkok?
N: Yes, I'm going to see a friend. And you?
E: I'm going to visit my father in Romania.

5 SG = Security Guard   W = woman

SG: Excuse me, you can't leave your bags here.
W: It's just for a minute. I'm going to use the toilet.
SG: Please take your bags with you.
W: I'm not going to take these big bags into the toilet!
SG: I'm sorry madam, but these are the rules.

12C Grammar exercise 3 🔵 2.86

1 W = woman   M = man

W: Anyway, this summer I'm going to visit my family. They're in France.
M: That sounds nice.
W: What about you? Are you going to travel next year?
M: Me? No, I'm not. I'm going to stay here.

2 M = man   W = woman

M: What are you going to do next Friday?
W: I don't have any plans. Why?
M: We're going to see the new Brad Pitt film. Would you like to come?
W: Yes, sure.

3 W = woman   M = man

W: Where are you going to go after class?
M: To the library. I'm going to study.

4 M = man   W = woman

M: Are you going to study English next year?
W: No, I'm not.
M: Oh no, why not?
W: I'm going to live in England. I've got a job there for next August.
M: Wow.

5 M = man   W = woman

M: Are you going to come to school tomorrow?
W: Yes! We're going to take the exam. Don't you remember?
M: Oh yes, that's right.

Irregular verb list

Infinitive	Past simple	Translation
be***	was/were	_____
become***	became	_____
break***	broke	_____
build***	built	_____
buy***	bought	_____
catch***	caught	_____
choose***	chose	_____
come***	came	_____
cost***	cost	_____
cut***	cut	_____
do***	did	_____
drink***	drank	_____
drive***	drove	_____
eat***	ate	_____
fall***	fell	_____
feel***	felt	_____
find***	found	_____
fly***	flew	_____
forget***	forgot	_____
get***	got	_____
give***	gave	_____
go***	went	_____
have***	had	_____
hear***	heard	_____
hit***	hit	_____
keep***	kept	_____
know***	knew	_____
learn***	learnt	_____
make***	made	_____
meet***	met	_____
pay***	paid	_____
put***	put	_____
read***	read	_____
ride**	rode	_____
run***	ran	_____
say***	said	_____
see***	saw	_____
sell***	sold	_____
send***	sent	_____
shut***	shut	_____
sit***	sat	_____
smell*	smelt	_____
speak***	spoke	_____
spend***	spent	_____
stand***	stood	_____
swim**	swam	_____
take***	took	_____
tell***	told	_____
win***	won	_____

Macmillan Education
Between Towns Road, Oxford OX4 3PP
A division of Macmillan Publishers Limited
Companies and representatives throughout the world

ISBN: 978-0-2300-2076-4 (with CD-ROM)
ISBN: 978-1-4050-1049-8

Original design by Oliver Design
Page make up by right on the line

Illustrated by Rowan Barnes-Murphy, page 46. Humbero Blanco, pages 66, 106. Fred Blunt, pages 99, 104, 105. Anne Cakebread, pages 7, 8 ,9, 11, 13, 15, 17, 19, 29, 33, 39, 51, 52, 53, 62, 64, 67, 70, 91, 105, 108, 109, 115, 116. Cyrus Deboo, pages 10, 30, 34, 40, 50, 52, 60, 66, 85, 96, 115, 119. Mark Duffin, pages 15, 16. Joanna Kerr, pages 11, 17, 26, 33, 35, 36, 45, 50, 52, 67, 85, 72, 115, 117. Peter Lubach, pages 13, 22, 30, 56, 91, 114, 119. Sarah Nayler, pages 7, 12, 27, 37, 56, 75, 87, 102, 105, 111.

Cover design by Macmillan Publishers Limited

Cover photography by: (from left to right) Corbis / Guenter Rossenbach / Zefa, Corbis / Bryan F. Peterson, Reuters / David Gray, Photolibrary / Jon Arnold Images, Corbis / Barry Lewis, Getty Images / Jeff Speed, Alamy / Jennie Hart, Reuters / Nguyen Huy Kham, Getty Images / Frans Lemmens, Getty Images / Bruno Barbier, Alamy / Travelstock 44.

Picture research by Sally Cole

Author's acknowledgements
I would like to thank the following teachers for their valuable suggestions and comments during the research of this book: Mark McKinnon at the Universidad Autonoma de Barcelona; Joaquin Gerardo from St Andrew's School, Elche; Duncan Foord at Oxford TEFL Barcelona; Whit Goodfellow and Patti Vora in Toronto.
Thanks to Robert Campbell and the team at iTs magazines who have had a profound influence on the way I write.
My heartfelt gratitude to Nick Sheard, Sue F. Jones and Katherine Stannett for all their help and support in developing the book. Thanks also to Katy Wright for her involvement in the early stages and to Philip Kerr for his constant encouragement.
Thanks to Elvira Lain and the students at the Angloalemana school of Elche for letting me try things out with them.
To Sofia, Lucas and Marcos: thank you for being there whenever I've needed you.

The author and publishers would like to thank the following people for their help and contribution:
Carolina Mussons, Mari-Carmen Lafuente, Eliseo Picó Mas, Carmen Roig-Papiol and Lourdes Montoro, EOI Sta Coloma de Gramanet, Barcelona. Maggie Hawes, Tony Isaac, Tom Radman and Anita Roberts, British Council, Barcelona. Rosie Dickson and Sarah Hartley, Merit School, Barcelona. Christina Anastasiadis, Andrew Graydon, Steven McGuire, Alan Hammans, Heather Shortland and Roger Edwards, International House Zurbano, Madrid. Guy Heath, British Council, Madrid. Ramón Silles, EOI Majadahonda. Javier Martinez Maestro, EOI Parla. Rosa Melgar, EOI Valdezarza. Susana Galan, The English Centre, Madrid. Yolanda Scott-Tennent Basallote, EOI Tarragona. Ceri Jones. Katherine Griggs.
Marzenna Raczkowska. Yaffite Mor, Alicja Fialek and Ricky Krzyzewski, UEC-Bell School of English, Warsaw. Steve Allen, Joanna Zymelka, Marek Kazmierski, Przemek Skrzyniarz, Colin Hinde, Mireille Szepaniak, Gabriela Pawlikowska and Simon Over, English First, Warsaw. Fiona Harrison-Rees, British Council, Warsaw. Karina Davies and Katarzyna Wywial, Szkola Jezykow Obcych 'Bakalarz', Warsaw. Peter Moran and Joanna Trojanowska, International House, Krakow. Walter Nowlan, British Council, Krakow. Agnieszka Bieniek, Anna Galus, Malgorzata Paprota and Joanna Berej, U Metodystow, Lublin. Mr Paudyna, Alicja Grajek, Eliza Trojanowska and Monika Bochyn'ska, Studium Jezykow Obcych, Minsk Mazowiecki. Paola Randali. Paola Povesi. Roberta Giugni. Mirella Fantin. Rossella Salmoiraghi. Marco Nervegna and Rebecca Kirby, Linguaviva, Milan. Peter Sheekey, Oxford Group, Milan. Irina Kuznetsova, Elena Ivanova, Olga Kekshoeva and Yulia Mukoseeva, Tom's House, Moscow. Asya Zakirova, Tatyana Tsukanova, Natalia Brynzynyuk, Anna Karazhas, Anastasia Karazhas and Nadya Shishkina, Mr English Club, Moscow. Inna Turchin, English First Zhulebino, Moscow. Tatiana Shepelenko, Ljuba Sicheva and Tatiana Brjushkova, Higher School of Economics, Moscow.
David Willis. Susan Hutchison. Kirsten Holt. Laila Meachin. Howard Smith, Clare Dunlop, Clare Waring and Andrew Mitchell, Oxford House, London. Garth Cadden, Lefteris Panteli and Vicky McWilliam, St Giles College, London. Sarah James, Sarah Lurie, Karen Mathewman, Chris Wroth, Olivia Smith, Sue Clark, Alan Greenslade-Hibbert, King's School of English, Oxford.
Sara Fiorini, CEFETI Centro de Linguas, São Paulo. Neide Silva and Maria Helena Iema, Cultura Inglesa Pinheiros, São Paulo. José Olavo de Amorim and Amini Rassoul, Colégio Bandeirantes, São Paulo. Maria Antonieta and Sabrina Teixeira, Centro Britânico, Perdizes

The authors and publishers would like to thank the following for permission to reproduce the following photographic material:
Alamy/travlestock 44 p14(l), Arcblue p17(b), Mode Images Ltd p17(tl), J. Tree p17(tr), S.May p17(mr), Lightworks Media p24(br), P.Talbot p32(C), J.Hart p34(br), R.Levine p38(tl), On Request Images p39, D.Crausby p44(F), J.Sullivan p48(l), OSO Media p60(br), B.Lawrence p61(bl), A.Linscott p64(t), Cephas PL p(B), B.Wymar p64(D), S.Saks p64(A), Pictorial Press Ltd p84(l), D.Pearson p90, Onrequest Images p92(b), A.Holt p98(t), T.Denson pp114(t),118(mt), Profimedia pp114(t),118(t), Camelot pp114(mb),118(mb); Axiom/C.Caldicott p79(l); Bridgeman Art Library/The "Fighting Temeraire" Tugged to her Last Berth to be Broken up, before 1839, Turner, Joseph Mallord William (1775-1851) / National Gallery, London, UK, P100, A Bar at the Folies-Bergeres, 1881-82 (oil on canvas), Manet, Edouard (1832-83) / © Samuel Courtauld Trust, Courtauld Institute of Art Gallery, P 100, Sunflowers, 1888, Gogh, Vincent van (1853-90) / National Gallery, London, UK, p100, Cafe Terrace, Place du Forum, Arles, 1888 (oil on canvas), Gogh, Vincent van (1853-90) / Rijksmuseum Kroller-Muller, Otterlo, Netherlands, P103(t); Corbis/P.Libera p8(F), G.Rossenbach p8(E), B. Lewis p8(G),G.Weiner p9(tl), Tobbe p12(t), D.Galante pp12 (m), 86(A), S.Hughes p12 (b), O.Eltinger p17(ml). P.Thompson p20(l),R.Kaufman p24(tr),R.Jensen/EPA p27, J.Raga p28(r), L.Christiansen p34(bl), G.Giglia p38(br), Benelux p42(B), K.Kulish p44(A), D.Tynan p47(bl), Z.Smith p47(tm), C.Karnow p61(tr), N.McGowan-Lowe p63,R.Folkks p74(b), D&J.Frent p81(m),J.Kurtz p82(A), Y.Liu p86(B), C.Savage p86(C), P.Steiner pp96(t),118(t), Bettmann p103(b), D.Ramazani p104, B.Peterson p110; Empics/M.Fernandez p9(tr), F.Llano p9(br); G.Galia p32(a), S.Galia pp34(tl),44,Getty/ F.Lemmens p6(br),C.Vasconellos p8(c), G.Hellier p8(A), O.Andersen p9(bl), J.Giustina p10, W.Ireland p19, I.Block p24(A), P.laCroix p24(D), F.Lemmens p26 (t), J.Bourke p26(b), U.Siostedt p28 (l), J.Sullivan p32(B), W.Eugene Smith p32(D), J.Grill p38(tr), D.Holloway p38(tr), C.Somodevilla p38(bl), T.Mosenfelder p38(ml), T.Werner p42(l), AFP p42(A), W.Maldonado p43, S.Olson p44(B), p44((D), J.Speed p47(tl), Altrendo Images p47(br), K.McMinimy p48(r), Getty Images p47(br), Widegroup p66(l), R.Estakhrian p66(r), L.Dutton p66(B), P.Weber p66(r), 98(b), Bongarts p69, D.Vervits p 73(l), J.James p73(r), B.Barbier p78, D.Neely p79(r), Hulton Archive p80, F.Chalfant p92(t), R. Estakhrian p102, M.Tama p108, LWA pp114(b), 118(b); Robert Harding p61(tl); Ronald Grant Archive/20th Century Fox p6(t), Paramount Pictures p6m, Woodfall Film Productions p6(bl), Warner Brothers p68(A),RKO p68 (B), Columbia Pictures p68 (D), ToHo p68 (E), Universal Pictures p68 (E); Photolibrary/P.Adams p8(H),D.Pearson p8(D), J.Arnold p14(r), J.Loic p44(c), B.Winsett p47(tr), A.Masterson p92(m); Rex Features pp42(background), 74(t), p66(A), S.Rosenlund p81(tr), N.Jorgensen p81(bl), R.Metzger p81(tl),(br); Science Photo Library/M.Thomas p25, SAE/Keystone USA p82(B); Reuters/N.Huykham p83, C.Sokunthea p84(r), D.Gray pp97,118(b); Tate Gallery/David Hockney Mr and Mrs Clark and Percy 1970-71 Acrylic on canvas 84 X120 © David Hockney© Tate London 2006. p101; Topfoto/D&J.Heaton, Topham Picturepoint p34(tr), T.Wiewandt pp50,51, J.Greenberg p93(l), T.Savino p96(b),118(m); Cartoonstock/M.Baldwin p38, G.Pilbrow p63; RF/Photodisc pp54(eggs),(fruit),(veg), soup, salad, BrandX p54(toast), C.King p54(milk), (ic-cream), Pixtal p54(chicken),(meat),(fish),Digital Vision p54(pasta).

Commissioned photography: David Tolley pp36,89, Peter Day p65, Rod Judges p88, John Cole pp93(A-H), 117(A-H);
The logos reproduced on p99 are published with the kind permission of: Greenpeace, Save the Children, Fairtrade and ICRC.
Lonely Planet guidebook published with permission from German Phrasebook © 2003, Lonely Planet Publications, p66(C).

Printed and bound in Spain by Edelvives
2011 2010 2009 2008 2007
10 9 8 7 6 5 4 3 2 1